ATTACK ON PEARL HARBOR, 1941

⊸⊶⧉⊷⊶

uncovered editions

Series editor: Tim Coates

Other titles in the series

View these titles at www.uncovered-editions.co.uk

uncovered editions

ATTACK ON PEARL HARBOR, 1941

CONCLUSIONS OF THE US CONGRESSIONAL COMMITTEE, 1946

∞⊱❈⊰∞

London: The Stationery Office

© The Stationery Office 2001

ISBN 0 11 702744 8

Extracts taken from *Investigation of the Pearl Harbor Attack, Report of the Joint Committee on the Investigation of the Pearl Harbor Attack*. Presented to the Congress of the United States on July 20, 1946.

A CIP catalogue record for this book is available from the British Library.

Cover photograph: President Franklin D. Roosevelt signs the Joint Congressional Resolution declaring a state of war between the US and Japan on December 8, 1941.
© Bettmann/CORBIS.

Typeset by J&L Composition Ltd, Filey, North Yorkshire.
Printed in the United Kingdom for The Stationery Office by Biddles Ltd, Guildford, Surrey.
TJ6142 C30 4/01

CONTENTS

About the series

Uncovered editions are historic official papers which have not previously been available in a popular form, and have been chosen for the quality of their story-telling. Some subjects are familiar, but others are less well known. Each is a moment in history.

About the series editor, Tim Coates

Tim Coates studied at University College, Oxford and at the University of Stirling. After working in the theatre for a number of years, he took up bookselling and became managing director, firstly of Sherratt and Hughes bookshops, and then of Waterstone's. He is known for his support for foreign literature, particularly from the Czech Republic. The idea for *uncovered editions* came while searching through the bookshelves of his late father-in-law, Air Commodore Patrick Cave OBE. He is married to Bridget Cave, has two sons, and lives in London.

Tim Coates welcomes views and ideas on the *uncovered editions* series. He can be e-mailed at tim.coates@theso.co.uk

At the beginning of December 1941, World War II had been fought for more than two years in Europe and in Asia. The United States was at this time still neutral, as it had been for much of World War I.

On the morning of Sunday December 7, 1941, without any declaration of war—indeed, while Japanese ambassadors were in Washington looking to resolve their differences with the US in the Pacific—the Japanese airforce repeatedly and virtually without any opposition bombed the US navy and air bases at Pearl Harbor on the island of Oahu, Hawaii, in the mid-Pacific. Totally unprepared for the attack, more than 2,000 people were killed, and a significant number of ships, planes, and other military equipment were completely destroyed. The next day, the US declared war on Japan, and three days later, on December 11, Japan's allies, Germany and Italy, declared war on the US. The war with Japan was finally concluded when atomic bombs were dropped by US planes on Hiroshima and Nagasaki in August 1945.

During the course of the war, several inquiries were held to investigate the disaster of Pearl Harbor. They focused on the military and intelligence weaknesses that allowed the destruction to take place. However, it was not until after the war had ended that evidence was presented which indicated that the cause of the lack of preparedness lay at more senior levels than had previously been suggested.

This book contains extracts from the report of that committee. Most notably it includes the additional views of Frank B. Keefe (representative from Wisconsin) and the minority report by senators Homer Ferguson and Owen Brewster, who concluded that among those most directly responsible for what happened were President Roosevelt and his closest advisers.

Attack on Pearl Harbor, 1941

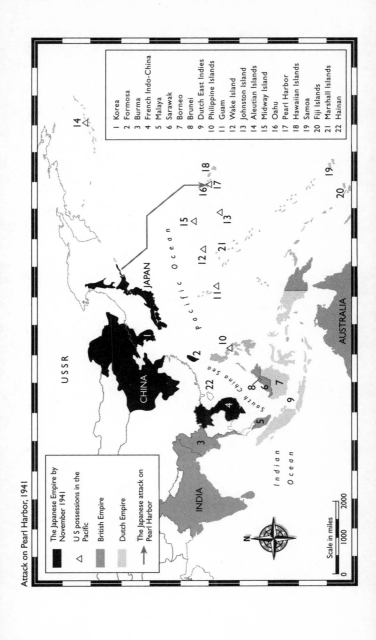

PART I

❦

THE JAPANESE ATTACK AND
ITS AFTERMATH

PHASES OF THE ATTACK
DECEMBER 7, 1941

Phase I: 7:55–8:25 a.m. Combined torpedo plane and dive bomber attacks

The beginning of the attack coincided with the hoisting of the preparatory signal for 8 o'clock colors. At this time (namely, 7:55 a.m.) Japanese dive bombers appeared over Ford Island, and within the next few seconds enemy torpedo planes and dive bombers swung in from various sectors to concentrate their attack on the heavy ships moored in Pearl Harbor. It is estimated that nine planes engaged in the attack on the naval air station on Ford

Deployment of attacking Japanese aircraft, December 7, 1941

First wave attack ordered — 07:50 a.m.

Second wave attack ordered — 08:50 a.m.

Japanese bombers

Japanese fighters

US airbase

US naval base

PACIFIC OCEAN

O A H U

Haleiwa

Wheeler Field

Pearl Harbor

Ewa

Ford Island

Hickham Field

Honolulu

Kaneohe

Bellows Field

0   10 km   10 miles

N

Oahu in the Hawaiian Islands

U.S.S.R.

China

Japan

Australia

Island and concentrated on the planes parked in the vicinity of No. 6 hangar.

At the time of the attack Navy planes (patrol flying boats, float planes, and scout bombers, carrier type) were lined up on the field. These planes caught fire and exploded. Machine-gun emplacements were set up hastily and manned, although the return fire from shore on Ford Island was pitifully weak. Then, as suddenly as they had appeared, the Japanese planes vanished. No further attack on this air station was made during the day. Except for a direct hit on No. 6 hangar resulting from a bomb which was apparently aimed at the battleship *California* and which fell short, the damage to the station itself was comparatively slight. However, 33 of the Navy's best planes out of a total of 70 planes of all types were destroyed or damaged.

As soon as the attack began, the commander of patrol wing 2 broadcasted from Ford Island the warning: "Air raid, Pearl Harbor. This is *not* drill." This warning was followed a few minutes later by a similar message from the Commander in Chief of the United States Fleet.

At approximately the same time that the Japanese dive bombers appeared over Ford Island, other low-flying planes struck at the Kaneohe Naval Air Station on the other side of the island. The attack was well executed, with the planes coming down in shallow dives and inflicting severe casualties on the seaplanes moored in the water. Machine guns and rifles were brought out, and men dispersed to fire at will at the low-flying planes. After a period of 10 to 15 minutes, the attacking planes drew off to the north at a low altitude and disappeared from sight. Several other contingents of bombers passed over, but none dropped bombs on Kaneohe Bay.

About 25 minutes after the first attack, another squadron of planes, similar to one of the Navy's light bomber types, appeared over Kaneohe and commenced bombing and strafing. No. 3 hangar received a direct hit during this attack and our planes in the hangar were destroyed. The majority of the casualties suffered at Kaneohe resulted from this attack. Most of the injured personnel were in the squadrons attempting either to launch their planes or to save those planes not as yet damaged. When the enemy withdrew, some 10 to 15 minutes later, salvage operations were commenced, but it was too late to save No. 1 hangar, which burned until only its steel structural work was left. Only nine out of the 36 planes at Kaneohe escaped destruction in this attack; six of these were damaged, and three were in the air on patrol south of Oahu.

Meanwhile, the Marine air base at Ewa was undergoing similar attack. Apparently the attack on Ewa preceded that at Pearl Harbor by about two minutes. It was delivered by two squadrons of 18 to 24 single-seater fighter planes using machine-gun strafing tactics, which came in from the northwest at an altitude of approximately 1,000 feet. These enemy planes would descend to within 20 to 25 feet of the ground, attacking single planes with short bursts of gunfire. Then they would pull over the tree-tops, reverse their course, and attack from the opposite direction.

Within less than 15 minutes, all the Marine tactical aircraft had been shot up or set on fire. Then the guns of the enemy fighters were turned upon Navy utility aircraft, upon planes that had been disassembled for repair, and upon the Marines themselves.

Effective defense measures were impossible until after the first raid had subsided. Pilots aching to strike at the enemy in the air viewed the wreckage which until a few minutes before had been a strong air group of Marine fighters and bombers. Altogether 33 out of the 49 planes at Ewa had gone up in smoke. Some Marines, unable to find anything more effective, had tried to oppose fighter planes with pistols, since the remaining 16 planes were too badly damaged to fly.

Although in phase I of the attack on the ships at Pearl Harbor Japanese dive bombers were effective, the torpedo planes did the most damage. They adhered strictly to a carefully laid plan and directed their attacks from those sectors which afforded the best avenues of approach for torpedo attack against selected heavy ship objectives. Thus they indicated accurate knowledge of harbor and channel depths and the berths ordinarily occupied by the major combatant units of the fleet. At least in the great majority of cases, the depth of water in Pearl Harbor did not prevent the successful execution of this form of attack. Shallow dives of the torpedoes upon launching were assured by the use of specially constructed wooden fins, remnants of which were discovered on enemy torpedoes salvaged after the attack.

Four separate torpedo plane attacks were made during phase I. The major attack was made by 12 planes, which swung in generally from the southeast over the tank farm and the vicinity of Merry Point. After splitting, they launched their torpedoes at very low altitudes (within 50 to 100 feet of the water), and from very short distances, aiming for the battleships berthed on the southeast side of Ford Island. All the outboard battleships (namely, the *Nevada*, *Arizona*, *West Virginia*, *Oklahoma*, and *California*) were effectively hit by one or more torpedoes. Strafing was simultaneously conducted from the rear cockpits. A recovered unexploded torpedo carried an explosive charge of 1,000 pounds.

During the second of these attacks, the *Oklahoma* was struck by three torpedoes on the port side and heeled rapidly to port, impeding the efforts of her defenders to beat off the attackers.

The third attack was made by one torpedo plane which appeared from the west and was directed against the light cruiser *Helena* and the minelayer *Oglala*, both of which were temporarily occupying the berth previously assigned to the battleship *Pennsylvania*, flagship of the Pacific Fleet. One torpedo passed under the *Oglala* and exploded against the side of the *Helena*. The blast stove in the side plates of the *Oglala*. Submersible pumps for the *Oglala* were obtained from the *Helena* but could not be used since no power was available because of damage to the ship's engineering plant.

The fourth wave of five planes came in from the northwest and attacked the seaplane tender *Tangier*, the target ship *Utah*, and the light cruisers *Raleigh* and *Detroit*. The *Raleigh* was struck by one torpedo, and the *Utah* received two hits in succession, capsizing at 8:13 a.m. At first it was feared that the *Raleigh* would capsize. Orders were thereupon given for all men not at the guns to jettison all topside weights and put both airplanes in the water. Extra manila and wire lines were also run to the quays to help keep the ship from capsizing.

The *Utah*, an old battleship converted into a target ship, had recently returned from serving as a target for practice aerial bombardment. As soon as she received her torpedo hits, she began listing rapidly to port. After she had listed to about 40 degrees, the order was given to abandon ship. This order was executed with some difficulty, as the attacking planes strafed the crew as they went over the side. Remnants of the crew had reached Ford Island safely. Later, knocking was heard within the hull of the *Utah*. With cutting tools obtained from the *Raleigh* a volunteer crew succeeded in cutting through the hull and rescuing a fireman, second class, who had been entrapped in the void space underneath the dynamo room.

An interesting sidelight on Japanese intentions and advance knowledge is suggested by the fact that berths F-10 and F-11, in which the *Utah* and *Raleigh* were placed, were designated carrier berths and that a carrier was frequently moored in nearby F-9.

The *Detroit* and *Tangier* escaped torpedo damage, one torpedo passing just astern of the *Detroit* and burying itself in the mud. Another torpedo passed between the *Tangier* and the *Utah*.

It is estimated that the total number of torpedo planes engaged in these four attacks was 21.

In the eight dive-bomber attacks occurring during phase I, three types of bombs were employed: light, medium, and incendiary.

During the second of these attacks, a bomb hit exploded the forward 14-inch powder magazine on the battleship *Arizona* and caused a ravaging oil fire, which sent up a great cloud of smoke, thereby interfering with antiaircraft fire. The battleship *Tennessee* in the adjacent berth was endangered seriously by the oil fire.

The *West Virginia* was hit during the third of these attacks by two heavy bombs as well as by torpedoes. Like the *California*, she had to be abandoned after a large fire broke out amidships. Her executive officer, the senior survivor, dove overboard and swam to the *Tennessee*, where he organized a party of *West Virginia* survivors to help extinguish the fire in the rubbish, trash, and oil which covered the water between the *Tennessee* and Ford Island.

The total number of dive bombers engaged in this phase is estimated at 30. While a few fighters were reported among the attackers in the various phases, they were no doubt confused with light bombers and accordingly are not treated as a distinct type.

Although the major attack by high-altitude horizontal bombers did not occur until phase III, 15 planes of this type operating in four groups were active during phase I.

Most of the torpedo damage to the fleet had occurred by 8:25 a.m. All outboard battleships had been hit by one or more torpedoes; all the battleships had been hit by one or more bombs with the exception of the *Oklahoma*, which took four torpedoes before it capsized, and the *Pennsylvania*, which received a bomb hit later. By the end of the first phase, the *West Virginia* was in a sinking condition; the *California* was down by the stern; the *Arizona* was a flaming ruin; the other battleships were all damaged to a greater or lesser degree.

Although the initial attack of the Japanese came as a surprise, defensive action on the part of the fleet was prompt. All ships immediately went to general quarters. Battleship ready machine guns likewise opened fire at once, and within an estimated average time of less than five minutes, practically all battleship and antiaircraft batteries were firing. The cruisers were firing all antiaircraft batteries within an average time of about four minutes. The destroyers, although opening up with machine guns almost immediately, averaged seven minutes in bringing all antiaircraft guns into action.

During this phase of the battle there was no movement of ships within the harbor proper. The destroyer *Helm*, which had gotten under way just prior to the attack, was just outside the harbor entrance when, at 8:17 a.m., a submarine conning tower was sighted to the right of the entrance channel and northward of buoy No. 1. The submarine immediately submerged. The *Helm* opened fire at 8:19 a.m., when the submarine again surfaced temporarily. No hits were observed.

Phase II: 8:25–8:40 a.m. Lull in attacks

This phase is described as a lull only by way of comparison. Air activity continued, although somewhat abated, with sporadic attacks by dive and horizontal bombers. During this phase an estimated total of 15 dive bombers participated in five attacks upon the ships in the navy yard, the battleships *Maryland*, *Oklahoma*, *Nevada*, and *Pennsylvania*, and various light cruisers and destroyers.

Although three attacks by horizontal bombers occurred during the lull, these appear to have overlapped into phase III and are considered under that heading.

At 8:32 a.m. the battleship *Oklahoma* took a heavy list to starboard and capsized.

During phase II there was still relatively little ship movement within the harbor. The ready-duty destroyer *Monaghan* had received orders at 7:51 a.m. (Pearl Harbor time) to "proceed immediately and contact the Ward in defensive in sea area." At about 8:37 a.m., observing an enemy submarine just west of Ford Island under fire from both the *Curtiss* and *Tangier*, the *Monaghan* proceeded at high speed and at about 8:43 a.m. rammed the submarine. As the enemy vessel had submerged, the shock was slight. The *Monaghan* thereupon reversed engines and dropped two depth charges.

The *Curtiss* had previously scored two direct hits on the conning tower. This submarine was later salvaged for inspection and disposal. The *Monaghan* then proceeded down the channel and continued her sortie. At the same time that the *Monaghan* got under way, the destroyer *Henley* slipped her chain from buoy No. X-11 and sortied, following the *Monaghan* down the channel.

Phase III: 8:40–9:15 a.m. Horizontal bomber attacks

The so-called "lull" in the air raid was terminated by the appearance over the fleet of eight groups of high-altitude horizontal bombers which crossed and recrossed their targets from various directions, inflicting serious damage. Some of the bombs dropped were converted 15- or 16-inch shells of somewhat less explosive quality, marked by very little flame.

According to some observers, many bombs dropped by high-altitude horizontal bombers either failed to explode or landed outside the harbor area.

During the second attack (at 9:06 a.m.) the *Pennsylvania* was hit by a heavy bomb which passed through the main deck amidships and detonated, causing a fire, which was extinguished with some difficulty.

The third group of planes followed very closely the line of battleship moorings. It was probably one of these planes that hit the *California* with what is believed to have been a 15-inch projectile equipped with tail vanes which penetrated to the second deck and exploded. As a result of the explosion, the armored hatch to the machine shop was badly sprung and could not be closed, resulting in the spreading of a serious fire.

Altogether, 30 horizontal bombers, including nine planes which had participated in earlier attacks, are estimated to have engaged in phase III. Once more it was the heavy combatant ships, the battleships and cruisers, which bore the brunt of these attacks.

Although phase III was largely devoted to horizontal bombing, approximately eight dive bombers organized in five groups also participated. It was probably the second of these groups which did considerable damage to the *Nevada*, then proceeding down the South Channel, and also to the *Shaw*, *Cassin*, and *Downes*, all three of which were set afire.

During the fifth attack, a Japanese dive bomber succeeded in dropping one bomb on the seaplane tender *Curtiss* which detonated on the main deck level, killing 20 men, wounding 58, and leaving one other unaccounted for. During this same phase, the *Curtiss* took under fire one of these bombers, which was pulling out of a dive over the naval air station. Hit squarely by the *Curtiss'* gunfire, the plane crashed on the ship, spattering burning gasoline and starting fires so menacing that one of the guns had to be temporarily abandoned.

Considerable ship movement took place during phase III. At 8:40 a.m. the *Nevada* cleared berth F-8 without assistance and proceeded down the South Channel. As soon as the Japanese became aware that a battleship was trying to reach open water they sent dive bomber after dive bomber down after her and registered several hits. In spite of the damage she had sustained in the vicinity of floating dry-dock No. 2, and although her bridge and forestructure were ablaze, the ship continued to fight effectively. At 9:10 a.m., however, while she was attempting to make a turn in the channel, the *Nevada* ran aground in the vicinity of buoy No. 19.

Meanwhile the repair ship *Vestal*, also without assistance, had gotten under way at about 8:40 a.m., had cleared the burning *Arizona*, and at about 9:40 a.m. anchored well clear northeast of Ford Island.

Soon after the *Nevada* and *Vestal* had cleared their berths, tugs began to move the *Oglala* to a position astern of the *Helena* at 10-10 dock. The *Oglala* was finally secured in her berth at about 9 a.m., but shortly thereafter she capsized.

At 8:42 a.m., the oiler *Neosho* cleared berth F-4 unaided and stood toward Merry Point in order to reduce fire hazard to her cargo and to clear the way for a possible sortie by the battleship *Maryland*.

Phase IV: 9:15–9:45 a.m. Dive bomber attacks

During phase IV an estimated 27 dive bombers conducted nine strafing attacks directed against ships throughout the entire harbor area. In all probability the planes were the same ones that had conducted previous attacks. These attacks overlapped by about 10 minutes the horizontal bomber attacks described in phase III.

Phase V: 9:45 a.m. Waning of attacks and completion of raid

By 9:45 a.m. all enemy planes had retired. Evading Navy aerial searches, both shore-based and from carriers at sea, the Japanese striking force retired to its home waters without being contacted by any American units.

An outline review of the Japanese attack on Army planes and installations is as follows:

Hickam Field
(Army planes at the time of the attack were lined up on the warming-up aprons three or four abreast with approximately 10 feet between wing tips, and approximately 135 feet from the tail of one plane to the nose of another.)

First attack (lasting about 10 minutes): At about 7:55 a.m. nine dive bombers attacked the Hawaiian Air Depot buildings and three additional planes attacked the same objectives from the northwest. Several minutes later nine additional bombers bombed Hickam Field hangar line from the southeast. Immediately thereafter, seven more dive bombers attacked the hangar line from the east.

Second attack (lasting between 10 and 15 minutes): At about 8:25 a.m. between six and nine planes attacked the

No. 1 Aqua System, the technical buildings, and the consolidated barracks. During and immediately after this bombing attack, Army planes on the parking apron were attacked with gunfire. About 8:26 a.m. a formation of five or six planes bombed the baseball diamond from a high altitude, possibly believing the gasoline storage system to be in that area.

Third attack (lasting about eight minutes): At 9 a.m. from six to nine planes attacked with machine-gun fire the technical buildings behind the hangar lines and certain planes which by then were dispersed. At about the same time from seven to nine planes bombed the consolidated barracks, the parade ground, and the post exchange.

Wheeler Field

(Army planes were parked in the space between the aprons in front of the hangars, generally in a series of parallel lines approximately wing tip to wing tip, the lines varying from 15 to 20 feet apart.)

First attack (lasting approximately 15 minutes): At 8:02 a.m. 25 planes dive-bombed the hangar lines; machine-gun fire was also employed during the attack.

Second attack (lasting less than five minutes): At 9 a.m. seven planes machine-gunned Army planes being taxied to the airdrome.

Bellows Field

(The P-40s were parked in line at 10 to 15 feet intervals; the reconnaissance planes were also parked in a line at slightly greater intervals.)

First attack: At 8:30 a.m. a single Japanese fighter machine-gunned the tent area.

Second attack (lasting about 15 minutes): At about 9 a.m. nine fighters machine-gunned the Army planes.

Haleiwa Field was not attacked and after 9:45 a.m. there were no further attacks on Army installations. The evidence indicates that a maximum of 105 planes participated in the attacks on the airfields, it being noted that some of the planes included in this number may have taken part in more than one attack.

Submarine phase

Prior to completion of the surprise attack the advance Japanese expeditionary force of submarines was under the command of the striking force commander, Admiral Nagumo. The precise movements of the participating submarines are not known, but it is believed that most of these units departed from Japanese home waters in late November and proceeded to the Hawaiian area by way of Kwajalein. A few of the submarines, delayed in leaving Japan, proceeded directly to Hawaii. The functions assigned to the submarines in operations order No. 1 were:

(a) Until X-day minus 3 some of the submarines were to reconnoiter important points in the Aleutians, Fiji, and Samoa, and were to observe and report on any strong American forces discovered.

(b) One element was assigned to patrol the route of the striking force in advance of the movement of that force to insure an undetected approach.

(c) Until X-day minus 5, the remaining submarines were to surround Hawaii at extreme range while one element approached and reconnoitered without being observed.

(d) On X-day the submarines in the area were to "observe and attack the American Fleet in the Hawaii area; make a surprise attack on the channel leading into Pearl Harbor and attempt to close it; if

the enemy moves out to fight, he will be pursued
and attacked."

With orders not to attack until the task force strike was
verified, the force of I-class submarines took up scouting
positions on the evening of December 6 in allotted patrol
sectors covering the waters in the vicinity of Pearl Harbor.
Between 50 and 100 miles off Pearl Harbor, five midget
submarines were launched from specially fitted fleet submarines as a special attacking force to conduct an offensive
against American ships within the harbor and to prevent
the escape of the Pacific Fleet through the harbor entrance
during the scheduled air raid. Available data indicates that
only one of the five midget submarines penetrated into
the harbor, discharging its torpedoes harmlessly. None of
the five midget submarines rejoined the Japanese force.

The I-class submarines maintained their patrols in the
Hawaiian area after the attack and at least one of the group
(the I-7) launched its aircraft to conduct a reconnaissance
of Pearl Harbor to ascertain the status of the American
Fleet and installations. In the event of virtual destruction
of the American Fleet at Pearl Harbor, the operation plan
provided that one submarine division or less would be
placed between Hawaii and North America to destroy sea
traffic. At least one submarine (the I-7) was dispatched to
the Oregon coast on or about December 13.

Withdrawal of the striking force

Upon completion of the launchings of aircraft at 7:15 a.m.,
December 7, the fleet units of the Japanese striking force
withdrew at high speed to the northwest. Plane recovery
was effected between 10:30 a.m. and 1:30 p.m., whereupon
the force proceeded by a circuitous route to Kure, arriving
on December 23. En route two carriers, two cruisers, and
two destroyers were detached on December 5 to serve as

reinforcements for the Wake Island operation. The midget submarine personnel were prepared for death and none expected to return alive.

All original plans called for the retiring force to strike at Midway if possible but this strike was not made, probably because of the presence of a United States task force south of Midway.

DAMAGE AND LOSSES INCURRED

Damage to United States naval forces and installations as a result of the attack

Of the vessels at Pearl Harbor on the morning of December 7, those that were either sunk or damaged are listed in the table overleaf.

The Navy and Marine Corps suffered a total of 2,835 casualties, of which 2,086 officers and men were killed or fatally wounded. Seven hundred and forty-nine wounded survived. None was missing.

A total of 92 naval planes (including five scout planes from the carrier *Enterprise*) were lost and an additional 31

Vessels sunk or damaged at Pearl Harbor.

Type	Name	Extent of damage
Battleships	*Arizona*	Sunk
	California	Sunk
	West Virginia	Sunk
	Oklahoma	Capsized
	Nevada	Heavily damaged
	Maryland	Damaged
	Pennsylvania	Damaged
	Tennessee	Damaged
Light cruisers	*Helena*	Heavily damaged
	Honolulu	Damaged
	Raleigh	Heavily damaged
Destroyers	*Shaw*	Heavily damaged
	Cassin	Heavily damaged (burned)
	Downes	Heavily damaged (burned)
Repair ship	*Vestal*	Badly damaged
Minelayer	*Oglala*	Sunk
Seaplane tender	*Curtiss*	Damaged
Miscellaneous Auxiliaries	*Utah*	Capsized

planes damaged. At the Ford Island Naval Air Station one hangar was badly damaged by fire and another suffered minor damage. A complete hangar, in which planes were stored, was destroyed at Kaneohe Naval Air Station along with the planes therein and the seaplane parking area was damaged. At the Marine base at Ewa a considerable amount of damage was suffered by material installations, machinery tentage, and buildings. Damage at the base to aircraft was extremely heavy inasmuch as the primary objective was aircraft on the ground, the attacks being made on individual aircraft by enemy planes using explosive and incendiary bullets from extremely low altitudes.

The Japanese attack on Pearl Harbor cannot be separated from the wide-scale operations of which it was a part. On the evening of December 7, Japanese forces struck Hong Kong, Guam, the Philippine Islands, Wake and, on the morning of December 8, Midway.

The vessels in Pearl Harbor included 8 battleships; 2 heavy cruisers; 6 light cruisers; 29 destroyers; 5 submarines; 1 gunboat; 8 destroyer minelayers; 1 minelayer; 4 destroyer minesweepers; 6 minesweepers; and 24 auxiliaries.

Units of the Pacific Fleet not in Pearl Harbor at the time of the attack included:

(1) Task Force 8 under Admiral Halsey, consisting of one aircraft carrier, the *Enterprise*, three heavy cruisers, and nine destroyers, was about 200 miles west of Oahu en route to Pearl Harbor after having ferried Marine Corps fighter planes to Wake Island.

(2) Task Force 12 under Admiral Newton, consisting of one aircraft carrier, the *Lexington*, three heavy cruisers, and five destroyers, was about 460 miles southeast of Midway en route to Midway from Pearl Harbor with a squadron of Marine Corps scout bombers.

(3) Task Force 3 under Admiral Wilson Brown, consisting of one heavy cruiser and five destroyer minesweepers, had just arrived off Johnston Island to conduct tests of a new type landing craft.

(4) Other units of the fleet were on isolated missions of one type or another.

Damage to United States Army forces and installations as a result of the attack

The Army suffered a total of 600 casualties, including 194 killed in action and 360 wounded. A total of 96 Army planes were lost as a result of enemy action, this figure including aircraft destroyed in depots and those damaged planes which were subsequently stripped for parts.

In addition, extensive damage was inflicted on Army installations as reflected by photographic evidence submitted to the Committee.

Japanese losses
It has been estimated, by our own sources, that the Japanese lost a total of 28 planes, most of them being dive bombers and torpedo planes, as a result of Navy action. Three Japanese submarines of 45 tons each, carrying two torpedoes, were accounted for; two were destroyed by Navy action; and one was grounded off Bellows Field and recovered. From reports available it is estimated that the Japanese lost, due solely to Navy action, a minimum of 68 killed. One officer, an ensign, was taken prisoner when he abandoned the submarine which grounded off Bellows Field.

General Short reported that 11 enemy aircraft were shot down by Army pursuit planes and antiaircraft fire.

Information developed through Japanese sources indicates, however, that a total of only 29 aircraft were lost and all of the five midget submarines.

Summary comparison of losses
As a result of the December 7 attack on Hawaii, military and naval forces of the United States suffered 3,435 casualties; Japan, less than 100. We lost outright 188 planes; Japan, 29. We suffered severe damage to or loss of 8 battleships, 3 light cruisers, 3 destroyers, and 4 miscellaneous vessels; Japan lost 5 midget submarines. The astoundingly disproportionate extent of losses marks the greatest military and naval disaster in our Nation's history. The only compensating feature was the many acts of personal valor during the attack.

In addition 22 were missing in action, 2 died (nonbattle), 1 was declared dead (Public Law 490), and 21 died of wounds.

PART II

∽☒∽

THE FINDINGS AS TO
RESPONSIBILITY

THE COMMITTEE'S REPORT

CONCLUSIONS

The December 7, 1941, attack on Pearl Harbor was an unprovoked act of aggression by the Empire of Japan. The treacherous attack was planned and launched while Japanese ambassadors, instructed with characteristic duplicity, were carrying on the pretense of negotiations with the Government of the United States with a view to an amicable settlement of differences in the Pacific.

The ultimate responsibility for the attack and its results rests on Japan. This was an attack that was well planned and skillfully executed. Contributing to the effectiveness of the attack was a powerful striking force, much more powerful than it had been thought the Japanese were able to employ in a single tactical venture at such distance and under such circumstances.

The diplomatic policies and actions of the United States provided no justifiable provocation whatever for the attack by Japan on this Nation.

The Secretary of State fully informed both the War and Navy Departments of diplomatic developments and, in a timely and forceful manner, clearly pointed out to these departments that relations between the United States and Japan had passed beyond the stage of diplomacy and were in the hands of the military.

The Committee has found no evidence to support the charges, made before and during the hearings, that the President, the Secretary of State, the Secretary of War, or the Secretary of the Navy tricked, provoked, incited, cajoled, or coerced Japan into attacking this Nation in order that a declaration of war might be more easily obtained from the Congress. On the contrary, all evidence conclusively points to the fact that they discharged their responsibilities with distinction, ability, and foresight and in keeping with the highest traditions of our fundamental foreign policy.

The President, the Secretary of State, and high Government officials made every possible effort, without sacrificing our national honor and endangering our security, to avert war with Japan.

The disaster of Pearl Harbor was the failure, with attendant increase in personnel and material losses, of the Army and the Navy to institute measures designed to detect an approaching hostile force, to effect a state of readiness commensurate with the realization that war was at hand, and to employ every facility at their command in repelling the Japanese.

Virtually everyone was surprised that Japan struck the fleet at Pearl Harbor at the time that she did. Yet officers, both in Washington and Hawaii, were fully conscious of the danger from air attack; they realized this form of attack on Pearl Harbor by Japan was at least a possibility; and they were adequately informed of the imminence of war.

Specifically, the Hawaiian commands failed:

(a) To discharge their responsibilities in the light of the warnings received from Washington, other information possessed by them, and the principle of command by mutual cooperation.

(b) To integrate and coordinate their facilities for defense and to alert properly the Army and Navy establishments in Hawaii particularly in the light of the warnings and intelligence available to them during the period November 27 to December 7, 1941.

(c) To effect liaison on a basis designed to acquaint each of them with the operations of the other, which was necessary to their joint security, and to exchange fully all significant intelligence.

(d) To maintain a more effective reconnaissance within the limits of their equipment.

(e) To effect a state of readiness throughout the Army and Navy establishments designed to meet all possible attacks.

(f) To employ the facilities, materiel, and personnel at their command, which were adequate at least to have greatly minimized the effects of the attack, in repelling the Japanese raiders.

(g) To appreciate the significance of intelligence and other information available to them.

The errors made by the Hawaiian commands were errors of judgment and not derelictions of duty.

The War Plans Division of the War Department failed to discharge its direct responsibility to advise the commanding general he had not properly alerted the Hawaiian Department when the latter, pursuant to instructions, had reported action taken in a message that was not satisfactorily responsive to the original directive.

The Intelligence and War Plans Divisions of the War and Navy Departments failed:

(a) To give careful and thoughtful consideration to the intercepted messages from Tokyo to Honolulu of September 24, November 15, and November 20 (the harbor berthing plan and related dispatches) and to raise a question as to their significance. Since they indicated a particular interest in the Pacific Fleet's base this intelligence should have been appreciated and supplied to the Hawaiian commanders for their assistance, along with other information available to them, in making their estimate of the situation.

(b) To be properly on the qui vive to receive the "one o'clock" intercept and to recognize in the message the fact that some Japanese military action would very possibly occur somewhere at 1 p.m. December 7. If properly appreciated, this intelligence should have suggested a dispatch to all Pacific outpost commanders supplying this information, as General Marshall attempted to do immediately upon seeing it.

Notwithstanding the fact that there were officers on 24-hour watch, the Committee believes that, under all the evidence, the War and Navy Departments were not sufficiently alerted on December 6 and 7, 1941, in view of the imminence of war.

RECOMMENDATIONS

Based on the evidence in the Committee's record, the following recommendations are respectfully submitted:

That immediate action be taken to insure that unity of command is imposed at all military and naval outposts.

That there be a complete integration of Army and Navy intelligence agencies in order to avoid the pitfalls of divided responsibility which experience has made so abundantly apparent; that upon effecting a unified intelligence, officers be selected for intelligence work who possess the background, penchant, and capacity for such work; and that they be maintained in the work for an extended period of time in order that they may become steeped in the ramifications and refinements of their field and employ this reservoir of knowledge in evaluating material received. The assignment of an officer having an aptitude for such work should not impede his progress nor affect his promotions. Efficient intelligence services are just as essential in time of peace as in war, and this branch of our armed services must always be accorded the important role which it deserves.

That effective steps be taken to insure that statutory or other restrictions do not operate to the benefit of an enemy or other forces inimical to the Nation's security and to the handicap of our own intelligence agencies. With this in mind, the Congress should give serious study to, among other things, the Communications Act of 1934; to suspension in proper instances of the statute of limitations during war (it was impossible during the war to prosecute violations relating to the "Magic" intelligence without giving the secret to the enemy); to legislation designed to prevent unauthorized sketching, photographing, and mapping of military and naval reservations in peacetime; and to legislation fully protecting the security of classified matter.

That the activities of Col. Theodore Wyman, Jr., while district engineer in the Hawaiian Department, as developed by the Army Pearl Harbor Board, be investigated by an appropriate committee of the Senate or the House of Representatives.

That the military and naval branches of our Government give serious consideration to the 25 supervisory, administrative, and organizational principles hereafter set forth.

Supervisory, administrative, and organizational deficiencies in our military and naval establishments revealed by the Pearl Harbor investigation

The Committee has been intrigued throughout the Pearl Harbor proceedings by one enigmatical and paramount question: "Why, with one of the finest intelligence available in our history, with the almost certain knowledge that war was at hand, with plans that contemplated the precise type of attack that was executed by Japan on the morning of December 7: Why was it possible for a Pearl Harbor to occur?"

The answer to this question and the causative considerations regarded as having any reasonably proximate bearing on the disaster have been set forth in the body of this report. Fundamentally, these considerations reflect supervisory, administrative, and organizational deficiencies which existed in our military and naval establishments in the days before Pearl Harbor.

In the course of the Committee's investigation still other deficiencies, not regarded as having a direct bearing on the disaster, have presented themselves. Otherwise stated, all of these deficiencies reduce themselves to principles which are set forth, not for their novelty or profundity, but for the reason that, by their very self-evident simplicity, it is difficult to believe they were ignored.

It is recognized that many of the deficiencies revealed by our investigation may very probably have already been corrected as a result of the experiences of the war. We desire, however, to submit these principles, which are grounded in the evidence adduced by the Committee, for the consideration of our Army and Navy establishments in the earnest hope that something constructive may be accomplished that will aid our national defense and preclude a repetition of the disaster of December 7, 1941. We do this after careful and long consideration of the evidence developed through one of the most important investigations in the history of the Congress.

1. Operational and intelligence work requires centralization of authority and clear-cut allocation of responsibility

Reviewing the testimony of the Director of War Plans and the Director of Naval Intelligence, the conclusion is inescapable that the proper demarcation of responsibility between these two divisions of the Navy Department did not exist.

War Plans appears to have insisted that since it had the duty of issuing operational orders it must arrogate the prerogative of evaluating intelligence; Naval Intelligence, on the other hand, seems to have regarded the matter of evaluation as properly its function. It is clear that this intradepartmental misunderstanding and near conflict was not resolved before December 7 and beyond question it prejudiced the effectiveness of Naval Intelligence.

In Hawaii, there was such a marked failure to allocate responsibility in the case of the Fourteenth Naval District that Admiral Bloch testified he did not know whom the commander in chief would hold responsible in the event of shortcomings with respect to the condition and readiness of aircraft.

The position of Admiral Bellinger was a wholly anomalous one. He appears to have been responsible to everyone and to no one. The pyramiding of super-structures of organization cannot be conducive to efficiency and endangers the very function of our military and naval services.

2. *Supervisory officials cannot safely take anything for granted in the alerting of subordinates*

The testimony of many crucial witnesses in the Pearl Harbor investigation contains an identical note:"I thought he was alerted"; "I took for granted he would under-stand";"I thought he would be doing that."

It is the same story—each responsible official seeking to justify his position by reliance upon the fallacious premise that he was entitled to rely upon the assumption that a certain task was being performed or to take for granted that subordinates would be properly vigilant. This tragic theme was particularly marked in Hawaii.

The foregoing was well illustrated in Admiral Kimmel's failure to appreciate the significance of dis-patches between December 3 and 6, advising him that Japanese embassies and consulates, including the embassy in Washington, were destroying their codes. Navy Department officials have almost unanimously testified that instructions to burn codes mean "war in any man's language," and that in supplying Admiral Kimmel this information they were entitled to believe he could attach the proper significance to this intelligence. Yet the Commander in Chief of the Pacific Fleet testified that he did not interpret these dispatches to mean that Japan con-templated immediate war on the United States.

That the Navy Department was entitled to rely upon the feeling that Admiral Kimmel, as a responsible intelli-gent commander, should have known what the burning of codes meant appears reasonable; but this is beside the point in determining standards for the future. The simple fact is that the dispatches were not properly interpreted. Had the Navy Department not taken for granted that Admiral Kimmel would be alerted by them but instead have given him the benefit of its interpretation, there could now be no argument as to what the state of alertness should have been based on such dispatches.

With Pearl Harbor as a sad experience, crucial intelligence should in the future be supplied to commanders accompanied by the best estimate of its significance.

3. Any doubt as to whether outposts should be given information should always be resolved in favor of supplying the information
Admiral Stark hesitated about sending the "one o'clock" intelligence to the Pacific outposts for the reason that he regarded them as adequately alerted and he did not want to confuse them. As has been seen, he was properly entitled to believe that naval establishments were adequately alert, but the fact is that one—Hawaii—was not in a state of readiness. This one exception is proof of the principle that any question as to whether information should be supplied to the field should always be resolved in favor of transmitting it.

4. The delegation of authority or the issuance of orders entails the duty of inspection to determine that the official mandate is properly exercised
Perhaps the most signal shortcoming of administration, both at Washington and in Hawaii, was the failure to follow up orders and instructions to insure that they were carried out. The record of all Pearl Harbor proceedings is replete with evidence of this fundamental deficiency in administration. A few illustrations should clearly demonstrate this fact.

In the dispatch of November 27, 1941, which was to be considered "war warning," Admiral Kimmel was instructed to "execute an appropriate defensive deployment preparatory to carrying out the tasks assigned in WPL-46."Very little was done pursuant to this order with a view to a defensive deployment; the Navy Department did nothing to determine what had been done in execution of the order. Yet virtually every responsible Navy Department official has testified as to what he "assumed" Kimmel would do upon receipt of this dispatch. While it appears to have been the policy to leave the implementation of orders to the local commander, as a matter of future practice it would seem a safer policy to recognize, as implicit in the delegation of authority or the issuance of orders, the responsibility of inspecting and supervising to determine that the delegated authority is properly administered and the orders carried out.

The story of Admiral Kimmel's administration of the Pacific Fleet and supervision of the Fourteenth Naval District as well as General Short's administration of the Hawaiian Department in the critical days before December 7 is the epitome of worthy plans and purposes which were never implemented. The job of an administrator is only half completed upon the issuance of an order; it is discharged when he determines the order has been executed.

5. The implementation of official orders must be followed with closest supervision

In the November 27 warning sent to General Short he was ordered "to undertake such reconnaissance and other measures as you deem necessary" and to "report measures taken."The commanding general reported: "Re your 472. Department alerted to prevent sabotage. Liaison with Navy."

This message from General Short was not clearly responsive to the order. Yet during the nine days before Pearl Harbor not one responsible officer in the War Plans Division of the War Department pointed out to the commanding general his failure to alert the Hawaiian Department consistent with instructions. As a matter of fact, it does not affirmatively appear that anyone upon receipt of General Short's reply "burdened" himself sufficiently to call for message No. 472 in order to determine to what the report was responsive.

6. *The maintenance of alertness to responsibility must be insured through repetition*

It has been suggested, in explaining why additional warnings were not sent to Admiral Kimmel and General Short, that it was desired to avoid crying "wolf" too often lest the department commanders become impervious to the significance of messages designed to alert them. The McCollum message, for example, was not dispatched for the reason that overseas garrisons were regarded as fully alerted. Admiral Noyes is alleged to have referred to the proposed dispatch as an insult to the intelligence of the commander in chief inasmuch as he felt Admiral Kimmel had received adequate information. Although the exact provisions of the McCollum dispatch are unknown, it would seem to have been a safer practice to have sent this additional warning to intensify and insure alertness over a period of time through repetition, particularly under the critical circumstances prevailing between November 27 and December 7, 1941.

No consideration appears to have been given to the thought that since nothing occurred for nine days after the warnings of November 27 there would be a lessening of vigilance by reason of the simple fact that nothing did occur for several days following such warnings. Of course, this observation has little or no application to the Hawaiian situation; for had Japan struck on November 28, the next day after the warnings, the same lack of readiness would substantially have prevailed as existed on the morning of December 7. There could have been no lessening of alertness there for the reason that the Hawaiian commands were at no time properly alert.

7. Complacency and procrastination are out of place where sudden and decisive action are of the essence

Beyond serious question Army and Navy officials both in Hawaii and in Washington were beset by a lassitude born of 20 years of peace. Admiral Kimmel admitted he was affected by the "peace psychology" just like "everybody else." As expressed by Admiral McMorris: "We were a bit too complacent there." The manner in which capable officers were affected is to a degree understandable, but the Army and the Navy are the watchdogs of the Nation's security and they must be on the alert at all times, no matter how many the years of peace.

As indicated in the body of this report, there was a failure in the War and Navy Departments during the night of December 6–7 to be properly on the qui vive consistent with the knowledge that the Japanese reply to our Government's note of November 26 was being received. The failure of subordinate officials to contact the Chief of Staff and Chief of Naval Operations on the evening of December 6 concerning the first 13 parts of the 14-part memorandum is indicative of the "business as usual" attitude. Some prominent military and naval officials were entertaining and, along with other officers, apparently failed to read into the 13 parts the importance of and necessity of greater alertness.

Of a similar tenor is the remark of Admiral Kimmel with respect to the "lost" Japanese carriers: "Do you mean to say that they could be rounding Diamond Head ?" Or the observation attributed to General Short with respect to the transcript of the "Mori" conversation that it looked quite in order and was nothing to be excited about.

The people are entitled to expect greater vigilance and alertness from their Army and Navy whether in war or in peace.

8. The coordination and proper evaluation of intelligence in times of stress must be insured by continuity of service and centralization of responsibility in competent officials

On occasion witnesses have echoed the sentiment that the Pearl Harbor debacle was made possible, not by the egregious errors or poor judgment of any individual or individuals, but rather by reason of the imperfection and deficiencies of the system whereby Army and Navy intelligence was coordinated and evaluated. Only partial credence, however, can be extended to this conclusion inasmuch as no amount of coordination and no system could be effected to compensate for lack of alertness and imagination. Nevertheless, there is substantial basis, from a review of the Pearl Harbor investigation in its entirety, to conclude that the system of handling intelligence was seriously at fault and that the security of the Nation can be insured only through continuity of service and centralization of responsibility in those charged with handling intelligence. And the assignment of an officer having an aptitude for such work over an extended period of time should not impede his progress nor affect his promotions.

The professional character of intelligence work does not appear to have been properly appreciated in either the War or Navy Departments. It seems to have been regarded as just another tour of duty, as reflected by limitations imposed on the period of assignment to such work, among other things. The Committee has received the distinct impression that there was a tendency, whether realized or not, to relegate intelligence to a role of secondary importance.

As an integrated picture, the Pearl Harbor investigations graphically portray the imperative necessity, in the War and Navy Departments: (1) for selection of men for intelligence work who possess the background, capacity, and penchant for such work; (2) for maintaining them in the work over an extended period of time in order that they may become steeped in the ramifications and refinements of their field and employ this reservoir of knowledge in evaluating data received; and (3) for the centralization of responsibility for handling intelligence to avoid all of the pitfalls of divided responsibility which experience has made so abundantly apparent.

9. The unapproachable or superior attitude of officials is fatal; there should never be any hesitancy in asking for clarification of instructions or in seeking advice on matters that are in doubt

Despite the fact that the record of testimony in the Pearl Harbor proceedings is filled with various interpretations as to what War and Navy Department dispatches meant, in not one instance does it appear that a subordinate requested a clarification. General Short was ordered to undertake reconnaissance, yet he apparently ignored the order assuming that the man who prepared it did not know of his special agreement—with the Navy in Hawaii whereby the latter was to conduct distant reconnaissance. He chose to implement an order which manifestly he did not understand, without the presumption that the man who prepared it did not know what he was doing, rather than request clarifying instructions.

On November 27 Admiral Kimmel received a message beginning with the words: "This dispatch is to be considered a war warning." Every naval officer who has testified on the subject has stated that never before in his naval experience had he ever seen a dispatch containing the words "war warning"; Admiral Kimmel testified that never before in his some 40 years as a naval officer had he seen these words employed in an official dispatch. In the same message there was another term, "defensive deployment," which the commander in chief manifestly did not clearly understand. In spite of his apparent uncertainty as to the meaning of the message, Admiral Kimmel, it can be presumed, chose to endeavor to implement it without seeking advice from the Navy Department.

While there is an understandable disposition of a subordinate to avoid consulting his superior for advice except where absolutely necessary in order that he may demonstrate his self-reliance, the persistent failure without exception of Army and Navy officers, as revealed by the investigation, to seek amplifying and clarifying instructions from their superiors is strongly suggestive of just one thing: That the military and naval services failed to instill in their personnel the wholesome disposition to consult freely with their superiors for the mutual good and success of both superior and subordinate. One witness, upon being asked why an explanation was not requested replied, in effect: "Well, I have found the asking is usually the other way"; that is, the superior asking the subordinate. Such a situation is not desirable, and the services should not be prejudiced by walls of "brass."

10. There is no substitute for imagination and resourcefulness on the part of supervisory and intelligence officials

As reflected by an examination of the situation in Hawaii, there was failure to employ the necessary imagination with respect to the intelligence which was at hand.

Washington, like Hawaii, possessed unusually significant and vital intelligence. Had greater imagination and a keener awareness of the significance of intelligence existed, concentrating and applying it to particular situations, it is proper to suggest that someone should have concluded that Pearl Harbor was a likely point of Japanese attack.

The Committee feels that the failure to demonstrate the highest imagination with respect to the intelligence which was available in Hawaii and in Washington is traceable, at least in part, to the failure to accord to intelligence work the important and significant role which it deserves.

11. *Communications must be characterized by clarity, forthrightness, and appropriateness*

The evidence before the Committee reflects an unusual number of instances where military officers in high positions of responsibility interpreted orders, intelligence, and other information and arrived at opposite conclusions at a time when it was imperative for them to estimate the situation and to arrive at identical conclusions.

Admiral Kimmel was ordered to execute an "appropriate defensive deployment." Everyone in Washington in testifying before the Committee seems reasonably certain as to just what this meant; Admiral Kimmel did not feel that it required his doing anything greatly beyond what he had already done, even though he knew that Washington knew what he had previously done. In using the words "this dispatch is to be considered a war warning" everyone in Washington felt the commander in chief would be sharply, incisively, and emphatically warned of war; Admiral Kimmel said he had construed the messages he had received previously as war warnings. Everyone in Washington felt that upon advising Hawaii the Japanese were destroying their codes it would be understood as meaning "war in any man's language"; Admiral Kimmel said that he did not consider this intelligence of any vital importance when he received it.

The War Department warned General Short that hostilities were possible at any moment, meaning armed hostilities; General Short felt that sabotage was one form of hostilities and instituted an alert against sabotage only. Washington ordered the commanding general to undertake reconnaissance; the latter took for granted that the War Department had made a mistake and proceeded in effect to ignore the order on the basis of this assumption. General Short was instructed to report the measures taken by him pursuant to departmental orders. He replied that his department was alerted against sabotage and that he had effected liaison with the Navy; the Director of War Plans saw the reply and took for granted the commanding general was replying to a different warning concerning subversive activities, at the same time suggesting that some of his subordinates may have interpreted the reply to mean that, in effecting liaison with the Navy, General Short had necessarily carried out the order to conduct reconnaissance. General Short said he thought the order given to Admiral Kimmel to execute a defensive deployment necessarily required distant reconnaissance; the commander in chief did not so interpret the order. Admiral Kimmel saw the warning General Short received and took for granted the Army would be on a full alert designed to protect the fleet base.

As has been seen, an objective consideration of the warnings received by the Hawaiian commanders indicates they were adequate. But on the basis of the disaster, in the future "adequacy" cannot be regarded as sufficient. Dispatches must be unmistakably clear, forthright, and devoid of any conceivable ambiguity.

The Committee feels that the practice, indulged by the Navy, of sending to several commanders an identical dispatch for action, even though the addressees may be located in decidedly different situations, is distinctly dangerous. In the preparation of messages to outposts the dispatch to a particular officer should be applicable to his peculiar situation. What may well be characterized as the "lazy" practice of preparing a single dispatch should be replaced by a more industrious and effective system, whereby a separate "individualized" dispatch is sent to each commander whose particular situation varies greatly from that of another commander, or there may be reason for him because of distance or other factors to believe so.

It is believed that brevity of messages was carried to the point of being a fetish rather than a virtue. Dispatches must be characterized by sufficient amplitude to be meaningful not only to the sender but beyond reasonable doubt, to the addressee as well.

12. There is great danger in careless paraphrase of information received and every effort should be made to inquire that the paraphrased material reflects the true meaning and significance of the original

To preserve the security of their own codes the War and Navy Departments followed the natural and proper practice of paraphrasing messages received. From a review of several messages as paraphrased the Committee is of the opinion that the utmost caution and care should be employed in preserving the original meaning of material. One classic example will serve to illustrate this point.

In replying to the War Department's directive of November 27, 1941, General Short said:

Re your 472. Department alerted to prevent sabotage. Liaison with Navy.

As paraphrased upon receipt at the War Department, this message read:

> Department alerted to prevent sabotage. Liaison with Navy re your 472.

It is to be recalled that the Army and Navy had entered into a special agreement at Hawaii whereby the Navy assumed responsibility for long-range reconnaissance. Therefore, having ordered General Short to undertake reconnaissance, a reasonable construction of his message as paraphrased would be that the commanding general, through liaison with the Navy, had made the necessary arrangements for reconnaissance as instructed in the War Department's warning of November 27. The message which Short actually sent, however, cannot so easily be afforded this construction. The seriousness of this matter lies in the fact that failure to conduct long-range recon-naissance at Hawaii was the prime factor responsible for the Army and Navy having been caught flat-footed. Conceivably, had the message as paraphrased not been mis-leading, the War Department might well have followed up on General Short's message, pointing out that he had failed to take the necessary action to alert his command.

13. Procedures must be sufficiently flexible to meet the exigencies of unusual situations

Reviewing the Pearl Harbor evidence there are, in both the War and Navy establishments, several illustrations of inflexible procedures that could not be or at least were not subjected to sufficient alteration to satisfy the exigencies of the situation. Everything seems perforce to have followed a grooved pattern regardless of the demands for distinctive action. The idea of proceeding "through channels" was carried to an extreme.

Among the best illustrations of this fact was the failure of Admiral Kimmel to advise Admiral Newton that the "war warning" had been received. Admiral Newton was departing from Pearl Harbor with some of the most vital units of the Pacific Fleet, yet because the table of organization indicated Admiral Brown to be Newton's superior, the commander in chief did not take it upon himself to insure that Newton was fully informed as to the critical situation between the United States and Japan, and relied upon the usual procedure whereby Brown would keep Newton advised of developments.

14. Restriction of highly confidential information to a minimum number of officials, while often necessary, should not be carried to the point of prejudicing the work of the organization

The "Magic" intelligence was preeminently important and the necessity for keeping it confidential cannot be overemphasized. However, so closely held and top secret was this intelligence that it appears the fact the Japanese codes had been broken was regarded as of more importance than the "information" obtained from decoded traffic. The result of this rather specious premise was to leave large numbers of policy-making and enforcement officials in Washington completely oblivious of the most pertinent information concerning Japan.

The Federal Bureau of Investigation, for example, was charged with combating espionage, sabotage, and un-American activities within the United States. On February 15, 1941, Tokyo dispatched to Washington a detailed outline as to the type of espionage information desired from this country. The FBI was never informed of this vital information, necessary to the success of its work, despite the fact that the closest liaison was supposed to exist among the FBI, Naval Intelligence, and Military Intelligence.

General Hayes A. Kroner, who was in charge of the intelligence branch of G-2, has testified that he at no time was permitted to avail himself of the Magic. And this despite the fact that to effectively perform his work he should have known of this intelligence and one of his subordinates, Colonel Bratton, was "loaned" to General Miles to distribute Magic materials to authorized recipients.

While, as previously indicated, it is appreciated that promiscuous distribution of highly confidential material is dangerous, it nevertheless should be made available to all those whose responsibility cannot adequately and intelligently be discharged without knowledge of such confidential data. It would seem that through sufficient paraphrase of the original material the source of the information could have been adequately protected. Certainly, as great a confidence could be placed in ranking officials of various departments and bureaus of the Government as in the numerous technicians, cryptographers, translators, and clerks required for the interception and processing of the Magic.

15. There is great danger of being blinded by the self-evident
Virtually every witness has testified he was surprised at the Japanese attack on Pearl Harbor. This was essentially the result of the fact that just about everybody was blinded or rendered myopic by what seemed to be the self-evident purpose of Japan to attack toward the south—Thailand, Malaysia, the Kra Peninsula, and perhaps the Philippines and Guam. Japan had massed ships and amphibious forces, had deployed them to the south, and had conducted reconnaissance in that direction. So completely did everything point to the south that it appears everyone was blinded to significant, albeit somewhat disguised, handwriting on the wall suggesting an attack on us elsewhere.

The advice of the Army lieutenant to the radar operators to "forget it," when they informed him of the approach of a large number of planes, appears to have been based on the self-evident assumption that the planes were Army or Navy craft on patrol or the expected B-17s due to arrive from the west coast.

16. Officials should at all times give subordinates the benefit of significant information

Before the Committee, Admiral Turner testified that he regarded an attack on Pearl Harbor as a 50–50 possibility. Assuming this to be correct, there can be little doubt, considering the position he held as Director of War Plans in the Navy Department, that he could have given the Commander in Chief of the Pacific Fleet the benefit of his conclusion had he been disposed to do so. As a matter of fact Admiral Turner had the principal hand in preparing the November 27 "war warning."

As has been seen, the orders contained in the war warning necessarily carried the implication of an attack from without; however, the dispatch did not reflect the likelihood of an attack upon the fleet with the degree of likelihood manifested by Admiral Turner in indicating to the Committee his estimate of the situation. Admiral Turner's position would be indefensible were his estimate based on any information or intelligence he may have possessed. It appears, on the other hand, that his conclusion was predicated on a rather long-standing impression in the Navy that an attack on our Pacific Fleet by Japan could be expected at one time or another. It is regarded as unfortunate, however, that Admiral Turner did not see fit to give to the Pacific Fleet the benefit of his conclusions outlined, with benefit of retrospection, in such detail before the Committee.

17. *An official who neglects to familiarize himself in detail with his organization should forfeit his responsibility*

It would seem that War and Navy Department officials both in Washington and Hawaii were so obsessed by an executive complex that they could not besmirch their dignities by "stooping" to determine what was going on, or more especially what was not going on, in their organizations. Examples should illustrate this observation.

Admirals Stark and Turner both have testified they "thought" the Commander in Chief of the Pacific Fleet was receiving the Magic intelligence. Yet in a period of over six months, with relations between the United States and Japan mounting in tenseness and approaching a crisis, neither of these ranking officers determined for a fact whether the fleet was receiving this information.

In the case of Hawaii, the evidence indicates failures on the part of the commanding general and the commander in chief to actually determine what was going on in their organizations. Additionally, in a command by mutual cooperation it was as important that Admiral Kimmel know what General Short was doing, and vice versa, as that he knew what the fleet itself was doing. But, as has been heretofore pointed out, neither of these officers really verified whether his assumptions concerning what the other was doing were correct.

18. *Failure can be avoided in the long run only by preparation for any eventuality*

The record tends to indicate that appraisal of likely enemy movements was divided into "probabilities" and "possibilities." Everyone has admitted that an attack by Japan on Pearl Harbor was regarded as at least a possibility. It was felt, however, that a Japanese movement toward the south was a probability. The over-all result was to look for the probable move and to take little or no effective precautions to guard against the contingency of the possible action.

While it appears satisfactorily established that it is the basic responsibility of an outpost commander to prepare for the worst contingency, it is believed that this premise has been applied more in theory than in practice. The military and naval branches of the Government must be continuously impressed by, and imbue their personnel with, the realization that failure can be avoided over an extended period of time only by preparation for any eventuality, at least when hostilities are expected.

19. Officials, on a personal basis, should never countermand an official instruction

On October 16, 1941, the Chief of Naval Operations sent to the Commander in Chief of the Pacific Fleet a dispatch concerning the resignation of the Japanese Cabinet, pointing out, among other things, that "since the US and Britain are held responsible by Japan for her present desperate situation there is also a possibility that Japan may attack these two powers." But on October 17, referring to this dispatch, Admiral Stark, in a letter to Admiral Kimmel, said: "Things have been popping here for the last twenty-four hours but from our dispatches you know about all that we do. Personally I do not believe the Japs are going to sail into us and the message I sent you merely stated the 'possibility'; in fact, I tempered the message handed to me considerably."

It appears to have been a generally accepted practice in the Navy for the Chief of Naval Operations to supplement official dispatches by correspondence of a quasi-personal nature.

Despite this fact, it is regarded as an extremely dangerous practice for the Chief of Naval Operations to express an opinion on a personal basis to an outpost commander which has the inevitable effect of tempering the import of an official dispatch. Were it not for the fact that Admiral Stark supplied the Commander in Chief of the Pacific Fleet highly pertinent and significant information after his letter of October 17 and before December 7, the manner in which he emasculated the October 16 dispatch would be inexcusable. However, as has been seen in this report, some of the most vital intelligence and orders relating to Japan were supplied from Hawaii during November and December of 1941.

20. Personal or official jealousy will wreck any organization
This principle is the result of the general impression obtained by the Committee concerning the relationship between the Army and the Navy as well as concerning certain intra-organizational situations which existed. The relationship, understanding, and coordination between the War Plans Division and the Office of Naval Intelligence were wholly unsatisfactory. The War Plans Division, particularly, appears to have had an overzealous disposition to preserve and enhance its prerogatives.

The whole story of discussions during 1941 with respect to unity of command is a picture of jealous adherence to departmental prerogatives and unwillingness to make concessions in the interests of both the Army and the Navy. The same comment is applicable to the near dispute between Admiral Kimmel and General Short as to which of them should command Wake and Midway when the Marines were replaced by soldiers. It is proper to suggest that, had both the commanding officers in Hawaii been less concerned between November 27 and December 7 about preserving their individual prerogatives with respect to Wake and Midway, and more concerned about working together to defend the Hawaiian Coastal Frontier in the light of the warnings they had received, the defensive situation confronting the Japanese on the morning of December 7 might well have been entirely different.

21. *Personal friendship should never be accepted in lieu of liaison or confused therewith where the latter is necessary to the proper functioning of two or more agencies*

One of the more "human" aspects of the testimony of both Admiral Kimmel and General Short is the manner in which each sought to bring out their personal friendship. For the purpose of demonstrating the close relationship that existed between them, Admiral Stark said: "I might point out, in passing, that there was nothing unusual in this so-called 'personal' correspondence between the Chief of Naval Operations and the commanders in chief—it was a long-established custom when I took office." They played golf together; they dined together; but they did not get together on official business in such a manner as to insure that each possessed the same knowledge of the situation as the other and to effect coordination and integration of their efforts.

22. *No considerations should be permitted as an excuse for failure to perform a fundamental task*

Both the commanding officers in Hawaii have offered, as explanation and excuse for failure to perform various supervisory and administrative responsibilities in their commands, the fact that they had countless and manifold duties in their respective positions as Commander in Chief of the Pacific Fleet and commanding general of the Hawaiian Department.

Additionally, Admiral Kimmel has referred to the extraordinarily competent staff which he had in Hawaii. The most fundamental responsibility that both commanders had under the circumstances, however, was to make certain beyond any reasonable doubt that there was an integrated and coordinated employment of defensive facilities consistent with the principle of command by mutual cooperation. No excuse or explanation can justify or temper the failure to discharge this responsibility which superseded and surpassed all others.

23. Superiors must at all times keep their subordinates adequately informed and, conversely, subordinates should keep their superiors informed

In Washington, Admiral Wilkinson, Director of Naval Intelligence, and Captain McCollum, Chief of the Far Eastern Section of that division, were not adequately and currently informed as to the nature of the dispatches being sent to our outposts emanating from the War Plans Division. Subordinate officials in both the War and Navy Departments failed to appreciate the importance and necessity of getting to both General Marshall and Admiral Stark the first 13 parts of the Japanese 14-part memorandum immediately on the evening of December 6. Colonel French did not inform the Chief of Staff that he had been unable to raise the Army radio in Hawaii on the morning of December 7. In Hawaii, Admiral Kimmel failed to insure that Admiral Bellinger, who was responsible for Navy patrol planes, knew of the war warning of November 27. Admiral Newton, as previously pointed out, was permitted to leave Pearl Harbor with a task force completely oblivious of any of the warning messages. General Short, construing the caution to disseminate the information in the warning of November 27 to "minimum essential officers" in a too-narrow manner, failed to inform the essential and necessary officers of his command of the acute situation in order that the proper alertness might pervade the Hawaiian Department.

24. The administrative organization of any establishment must be designed to locate failures and to assess responsibility

The Committee has been very much concerned about the fact that there was no way in which it could be determined definitely that any individual saw a particular message among the Magic materials. It does not appear that any record system was established for initialing the messages or otherwise fixing responsibility. The system existing left subordinate officers charged with the duty of disseminating the Magic at the complete mercy of superior officers with respect to any question as to whether a particular message had been delivered to or seen by them.

25. In a well-balanced organization there is close correlation of responsibility and authority

Witnesses have testified rather fully as to what their responsibilities were, both in Washington and at Hawaii. However, it does not appear that any of them, except the highest ranking officers, possessed any real authority to act in order decisively to discharge their responsibilities. It cannot be presumed that it will be possible to meet the exigencies of an emergency if the officer charged with the duty of acting at the time the emergency arises does not possess the necessary authority to follow through on the situation. There should be a close correlation between responsibility and authority; to vest a man with responsibility with no corresponding authority is an unfair, ineffective, and unsatisfactory arrangement.

ALBEN W. BARKLEY, *Chairman*
JERE COOPER, *Vice Chairman*
WALTER F. GEORGE
SCOTT W. LUCAS
J. BAYARD CLARK

JOHN W. MURPHY
BERTRAND W. GEARHART
FRANK B. KEEFE (*with additional views*)
(Senators Brewster and Ferguson are filing minority views)

ADDITIONAL VIEWS OF MR KEEFE

INTRODUCTION

Scattered throughout the whole of the committee report
are conclusions with respect to individuals in charge of
carrying out our diplomatic, military, and naval obligations
prior to the attack on Pearl Harbor. I find myself in
agreement with most of these conclusions and recommendations. The voluminous facts contained in the
committee report have been accurately assembled from the
enormous record compiled by the Committee. Any

criticism which I may have toward the marshaling of facts in the committee report is directed to the manner in which such facts have been used to sustain the various arguments and conclusions indulged in in the committee report.

It correctly states that both Washington and Hawaii were surprised at the attack upon Pearl Harbor. It is apparently agreed that both Washington and Hawaii expected the initial attack to come in the Asiatic area. What was done in Washington as well as what was done in Hawaii was admittedly done in the light of the universal military belief that Hawaii was not in danger from an initial attack by Japan. If this belief was unjustified, as I believe it was, then the mistake lies on the Washington doorstep just as much as it does upon that of Hawaii.

Throughout the long and arduous sessions of the Committee in the preparation of the committee report, I continuously insisted that whatever "yardstick" was agreed upon as a basis for determining responsibilities in Hawaii, it should be applied to the high command at Washington. This indicates in a general way my fundamental objection to the committee report. I feel that facts have been martialed [sic], perhaps unintentionally, with the idea of conferring blame upon Hawaii and minimizing the blame that should properly be assessed at Washington.

A careful reading of the committee report would indicate that the analysis of orders and dispatches is so made as to permit criticism of our commands in Hawaii while at the same time proposing a construction which would minimize the possibility of criticism of those in charge at Washington.

I think it is true that none of the military chiefs at Washington or Hawaii thought the attack would come at Pearl Harbor. I conclude that they all thought it would come first in the Far East. Obviously this was a fatal mistake, and I agree that the mistake was without proper justification and that neither Hawaii nor Washington should be excused from criticism for having made it. I think that the facts in this record clearly demonstrate that Hawaii was always the No. 1 point of danger and that both Washington and Hawaii should have known it at all times and acted accordingly. Consequently I agree that the high command in Hawaii was subject to criticism for concluding that Hawaii was not in danger.

However, I must insist that the same criticism with the same force and scope should apply to the high command in Washington. It is in this respect that I think the tenor of the committee report may be subject to some criticism.

I fully agree with the doctrine relating to the placing of responsibility in military officers in the field and their resulting duty under such responsibilities. I agree that they must properly sustain this burden in line with the high and peculiar abilities which originally gave them their assignments.

In the execution of their vitally important duties, however, the officers at the front in the field are fairly entitled to all aids and help and all information which can reasonably be sent to them from the all-powerful high staff command in Washington. If both commands are in error, both should be blamed for what each should have done and what each failed to do respectively. The committee report, I feel, does not with exactitude apply the same yardstick in measuring responsibilities at Washington as has been applied to the Hawaiian commanders. I cannot suppress the feeling that the committee report endeavors to throw as soft a light as possible on the Washington scene.

In order to clearly appraise the contentions herein expressed, I feel compelled to restate some of the basic military aspects of the Pearl Harbor disaster as shown by the evidence.

MILITARY ASPECTS OF THE PEARL HARBOR DISASTER

During the year 1941 the United States Pacific Fleet was based in Pearl Harbor in the Hawaiian island of Oahu. It had proceeded to the Hawaiian area for fleet exercises in the spring of 1940. Its scheduled return to its regular bases on the west coast was delayed from time to time. From these delays there gradually emerged evidence of the President's decision to retain the fleet in the Hawaiian area, to deter Japan from aggression in the Far East. The Commander in Chief of the Fleet, Admiral J. O. Richardson, protested this decision with a vigor which caused him to be relieved of command. He believed that the readiness of men and ships of the fleet for war operations would impress Japan rather than its presence in Hawaii, where facilities to render it ready for war were greatly inferior to those available on the west coast.

Richardson was succeeded in command by Admiral H. E. Kimmel in February 1941. The appointment of Kimmel was made on his record as a capable officer. There was no political or other favoritism involved. At this time the decision to base the fleet in Hawaii was an established fact. Pearl Harbor was the only anchorage in the Hawaiian area offering any security. It was then, however, an extremely deficient fleet base. Its exposed position rendered concealment of fleet movements practically impossible in an area filled with Japanese agents. The Army's equipment for anti-aircraft defense was meager. The local Army–Navy defense forces did not have sufficient long-range patrol planes to perform effective distant reconnaissance, even if the patrol planes of the fleet were made available to augment the handful of Army reconnaissance planes.

Under these circumstances, the position of the fleet in the Hawaiian area was inherently untenable and dangerous.

The fleet would sacrifice its preparations for war, and its potential mobility in war, if it concentrated its resources on the defense of its base. Moreover, with only four tankers suitable for fueling ships at sea, ships of the fleet had to come into Pearl Harbor for refueling, to say nothing of maintenance and repair, and the necessary rest and relaxation of crews.

Once the ships were in Pearl Harbor, with its single channel, they were a target for any successfully launched air attack from carrier-borne planes. The severity of the attack might be mitigated, but damage to the ships found in port was inevitable. To prevent a hostile carrier from successfully launching planes required that it be first discovered and attacked. Discovery, other than by lucky accident, required air reconnaissance of the perimeter of a circle of 800-mile radius from Oahu. The fleet did not at any time have patrol planes sufficient in number to carry out such reconnaissance. The Japanese task force which raided Oahu on December 7, 1941, was composed of six carriers. The Pacific Fleet had on that date three carriers, one of which was on the Pacific coast for repair, leaving only two immediately available in the area of a prospective sea engagement. An engagement at sea would have found the preponderant strength with Japan.

Although the fleet was placed by the President in the Hawaiian area in 1940 as an implement of diplomacy and as a deterrent to Japan, its strength was appreciably reduced in April and May of 1941. At that time, one aircraft carrier, three battleships, four cruisers, and 18 destroyers were detached from the Pacific Fleet and transferred to the Atlantic. The President directed the Chief of Naval Operations to consult the British Chiefs of Staff on the proposal to effect this transfer. They gave their opinion "that the consequential reduction in the strength of the United States Pacific Fleet would not unduly encourage

Japan" (letter from Admiral Danckwerts to Admiral Turner, April 28, 1941).

The transfer to the Atlantic was then carried out. The Commander in Chief of the United States Pacific Fleet was not asked for his opinion. The Chief of Naval Operations wrote him about the proposed transfer stating: "I am telling you, not arguing with you" (letter from Admiral Stark to Admiral Kimmel, dated April 19, 1941).

The primary mission assigned the Pacific Fleet under existing Navy War Plans was the making of raids on the Marshalls. These were to divert Japanese strength from the so-called Malay barrier. No existing War Plan of the United States in 1941 contemplated that the Pacific Fleet would go to the rescue of the Philippines or resist Japanese naval forces attacking the Philippines.

The Pacific Fleet was so inferior to the Japanese Navy in every category of fighting ship that such a mission was considered too suicidal to attempt. The American public in 1941 was deluded about the fighting strength of our fleet in the Pacific, by irresponsible utterances from men in authority.

Japan was under no such misconception. Her consular agents in the Hawaiian islands needed only their eyesight, and possibly binoculars, to appraise correctly the strength of the fleet.

An inferior fleet, under enemy surveillance in an exposed naval base without resources to protect it, could only avert disaster by receiving the best possible evidence of the intentions of its potential enemy. The Commander in Chief of the Fleet in 1941 recognized that that information was essential to his making appropriate dispositions to meet any crisis. He formally requested the Chief of Naval Operations that he "be immediately informed of all important developments as they occur and by the quickest secure means available."

The best evidence of Japanese intentions in the year 1941, available to the United States Government, were messages exchanged between the Government of Japan and her diplomatic consular agents abroad. These were intercepted by the Army and Navy. These were decoded and translated in Washington. The President, the Secretaries of State, War, and Navy, the Chief of Staff, and the Chief of Naval Operations regularly received these intercepted messages.

The President and the other officials receiving the intercepted messages in Washington prior to December 7, 1941, considered it likely that Japan would attack the United States. At a meeting of the President and his so-called War Council on November 25, 1941, according to Mr Stimson's notes the President stated: "that we were likely to be attacked perhaps (as soon as) next Monday." There was abundant evidence in the intercepted messages that Japan intended to attack the United States; Japan had fixed a dead-line date of November 25, extended to November 29, for reaching a diplomatic agreement with the United States. There were at least six Japanese messages emphasizing this dead-line. If the dead-line date passed without agreement, the Japanese Government advised her ambassadors in Washington: "Things are automatically going to happen." The necessity for agreement by the dead-line date was stressed by Japan in these terms: "The fate of our Empire hangs by the slender thread of a few days"; "We gambled the fate of our land on the throw of this die." On November 26, 1941, prior to the advanced "dead-line" date, the United States Government delivered to Japan a diplomatic note which the intercepted messages revealed Japan considered to be a "humiliating proposal," impossible of acceptance. The intercepted diplomatic messages further revealed that Japan expected to "rupture" negotiations with the United States when she replied to the American note of November 26. To prevent the United States from becoming unduly suspicious, Japan instructed her envoys in Washington to keep up a pretext of continuing negotiations until this Japanese reply was ready for delivery. A message from the Japanese Government to its ambassador in Berlin, sent on November 30, was intercepted and translated by the Navy in Washington on December 1.

In this message the Japanese Ambassador was instructed to:

> immediately interview Chancellor Hitler and Foreign Minister Ribbentrop and confidentially communicate to them a summary of developments. Say very secretly to them that there is extreme danger that war may suddenly break out between the Anglo-Saxon nations and Japan through some clash of arms and add the time of the breaking out of this war may come quicker than anyone dreams.

The President regarded this message as of such interest that he retained a copy of it, contrary to the usual practice in handling the intercepted messages. On December 2, 1941 elaborate instructions from Japan were intercepted dealing in precise detail with the method of internment of American and British nationals in Asia "on the outbreak of war with England and the United States."

In the "bomb plot" or "ships in harbor" message of September 24 the Japanese Government gave detailed instructions to its consul general in Hawaii as to the character of report it required concerning vessels in Pearl Harbor. Pearl Harbor was to be divided into five sub-areas. An alphabetical symbol was given each area. The Japanese government instructed the consul:

With regard to warships and aircraft carriers, we would like to have you report on those at anchor (these are not so important), tied up at wharves, buoys, and in the docks. (Designate types and classes briefly.) If possible we would like to have you make mention of the fact when there are two or more vessels alongside the same wharf.

This dispatch was decoded and translated in Washington on October 9, 1941.

On September 29, 1941, the Japanese consul in Hawaii replied to his Government. He established a system of symbols to be used in designating the location of vessels at key points in Pearl Harbor. This dispatch was decoded and translated in Washington on October 10, 1941.

On November 15, 18, 20, and 29 the Japanese Government urgently called for information about the location of ships in Pearl Harbor. On November 15 the Japanese consul in Honolulu was directed to make his "ships in harbor report" irregular but at the rate of twice a week. The reports were to give vessel locations in specific areas of the harbor, using the symbols established in September. The greatest secrecy was enjoined, because relations between Japan and the United States were described as "most critical." On November 18, the Japanese consul general reported to Tokyo the locations of the ships in the various sub-areas of Pearl Harbor, giving minute descriptions of the courses, speed, and distances apart of destroyers entering the harbor. On November 29 reports were requested even though there were no movements of ships. These dispatches were intercepted, decoded, and translated in Washington on December 3, 4, 5, and 6, 1941.

The "bomb plot" or "ships in harbor" message, and those messages relating to Pearl Harbor which followed it, meant that the ships of the Pacific Fleet in Pearl Harbor were marked for a Japanese attack. No other American harbor was divided into sub-areas by Japan. In no other area did Japan seek information as to whether two or more vessels were alongside the same wharf. Prior to this message Japanese espionage in Hawaii was directed to ascertain the general whereabouts of the American fleet, whether at sea or in port. With this message Japan inaugurated a new policy directed to Pearl Harbor and to no other place, in which information was no longer sought merely as to the general whereabouts of the fleet, but as to the presence of particular ships in particular areas of the harbor. In the period immediately preceding the attack Japan required such reports even when there was no movement of ships in and out of Pearl Harbor. The reports which Japan thus sought and received had a useful purpose only in planning and executing an attack upon the ships in port. These reports were not just the work of enthusiastic local spies gathering meticulous details in an excess of zeal. They were the product of instructions emanating from the Government of Japan in Tokyo.

Officers of the high command in Washington have admitted before us that this message, if correctly evaluated, meant an attack on ships of the Pacific Fleet in Pearl Harbor.

Lieutenant Commander Kramer of Naval Intelligence in Washington promptly distributed the Pearl Harbor "bomb plot" message to the President, the Secretary of the Navy, the Chief of Naval Operations, Admiral Stark, the Director of Naval Communications, the Director of War Plans, and the Director of Naval Intelligence. It bore the notation "interesting message." It was accompanied by a summary of its contents as follows:

Tokyo directs special reports on ships in Pearl Harbor which is divided into five areas for the purpose of showing exact locations.

Military Intelligence through Colonel Bratton delivered the "bomb plot" message to the Secretary of War, the Chief of Staff, and the Chief of the War Plans Division. The message was discussed several times by Colonel Bratton, Chief of the Far Eastern section, Military Intelligence Division, War Department General Staff, with his opposite numbers in the Navy Department. They discussed the possible significance of the message, as indicating a plan for an air attack on ships in Pearl Harbor. In the course of these discussions officers in Naval Intelligence stated that the Japanese were wasting their time in getting such meticulous detail about the location of ships in Pearl Harbor because the fleet would not be in Pearl Harbor when the emergency arose. Despite the fact that the "bomb plot" message and related intercepts dealing with the berthing of ships in Pearl Harbor were delivered to General Marshall and Admiral Stark, they testified before the Committee that they have no recollection of ever seeing them. No intimation of these messages was given to General Short or Admiral Kimmel in Hawaii. On the contrary, Admiral Kimmel had been advised by the Navy Department on February 1, 1941:

> no move against Pearl Harbor appears imminent or
> planned for in the foreseeable future.

In the days immediately preceding Pearl Harbor, Japan made no effort to conceal the movements or presence of her naval forces in Southeast Asia. The movements of her troops in Indo-China at that time were the subject of diplomatic exchanges between the United States and Japan. Yet, the intercepts showed that some Japanese plan went into effect automatically on November 29 from which Japan hoped to divert American suspicion by a pretext of continued negotiations. What was its nature?

Only the President and his top advisers in Washington had this information.

Despite the elaborate and labored arguments in the report and despite the statements of high-ranking military and naval officers to the contrary, I must conclude that the intercepted messages received and distributed in Washington on the afternoon and evening of December 6 and the early hours of December 7, pointed to an attack on Pearl Harbor:

1. The "pilot message." This was a message from Japan to her ambassadors in Washington advising them that the Japanese reply to the American note of November 26 was ready and being sent to them in 14 parts; that it was to be treated with great secrecy pending instructions as to the time of its delivery, and that the time for its delivery was to be fixed in a separate message.

2. The first 13 parts of the Japanese reply. This included all but the last paragraph of the Japanese note handed to the Secretary of State on December 7.

3. The fourteenth and last paragraph of the Japanese reply, and the message to the Japanese ambassadors which fixed the time for delivery of the Japanese note as 1 p.m. Washington time, December 7.

The "pilot message" was filed in Tokyo at 6:56 a.m. Washington time, December 6, it was intercepted by the Navy by 7:20 a.m. Washington time, December 6 and forwarded to the Navy Department. It was sent by the Navy to the Army for decryption and translation about noon Washington time, on December 6. It was decrypted, translated, and distributed about 3 p.m. Washington time by the Army to Mr Hull, Mr Stimson, General Marshall, the Chief of the War Plans Division, General Gerow, and the Chief of Military Intelligence General Miles. In the

Navy Department the Director of Naval Intelligence, Admiral Wilkinson, received the so-called pilot message prior to 6 p.m. Washington time, December 6. He had previously told his subordinates to be on the lookout for the Japanese reply and felt sure that he gave instructions that the pilot message was to be delivered to Admiral Stark. Admiral Turner, Chief of the War Plans Division in the office of the Chief of Naval Operations, received the pilot message in the evening of December 6. Admiral Stark and General Marshall each deny that on December 6 he had knowledge of the pilot message. We find on the testimony of General Miles and Colonel Bratton that the pilot message was delivered to General Marshall during the afternoon of December 6, 1941.

This pilot message said that Japan's reply to the American note of November 26 was about to be sent from Tokyo to Washington, and indicated that a rupture of diplomatic relations or war was a matter of hours.

On the evening of December 6, between 9 p.m. and midnight, Washington time, the first 13 parts of the Japanese reply to the United States were delivered to the President, Mr Knox, the office of the Secretary of State, and the Chiefs of Army and Navy Intelligence. After reading this message the President stated: "This means war." He later telephoned Admiral Stark about the critical turn of events. When Mr Knox received the message he called Mr Stimson and Mr Hull and arranged a conference with them for Sunday morning.

Mr Stimson asked the Navy Department on Saturday evening to furnish him by 9 a.m. Sunday morning the following information:

> Compilation of men-of-war in Far East, British, American, Japanese, Dutch, Russian; also compilation of American men-of-war in the Pacific Fleet, without locations, and a

list of American men-of-war in the Atlantic without
locations.

Admirals Stark, Ingersoll and the Secretary of the Navy
were consulted about this request. The Secretary of the
Navy directed that the information be compiled and
delivered prior to 10 o'clock, Sunday December 7. This
was done. The compilation showed that practically all the
ships of the Pacific Fleet were in Pearl Harbor.

In the early morning of December 7, 1941, about 5
a.m., Washington time, the message fixing the hour for
delivery of the Japanese note as 1 p.m. Washington time
was available in the Navy Department in Washington. This
was eight and one-half hours before the attack on Pearl
Harbor. Admiral Stark and his principal subordinates have
testified before us that they had knowledge of this message
about 10:30 a.m. This was five and one-half hours after it
had been received in the Navy Department. It was about
three hours before the attack. The relation of p.m.
Washington time to early morning in Hawaii was pointed
out to Admiral Stark. Admiral Stark was urged by the
Director of Naval Intelligence to send a warning to the
fleet. The chief intelligence officers of the Army had the
"1 p.m. message" by 9 a.m. Washington time, immediately
appreciated its significance, but did not succeed in bringing it to General Marshall's attention until nearly several
hours later. Marshall was horseback riding in Virginia. No
action was taken by the Army until he saw and read the
1 p.m. message and related intercepts, at which time he
sent a message to General Short which went over commercial facilities and was received after the Pearl Harbor
attack. Admiral Stark took no action on this information
except to agree to the inclusion in the belated Army message of instructions to General Short to advise Admiral
Kimmel of its contents.

Mr Hull, Mr Stimson, and Mr Knox had the 1 p.m. message at their conference about 10:30 a.m. Washington time December 7. The relation of Washington time to time in Hawaii and the Philippines was brought to their attention. Mr Stimson's notes describing the Sunday morning conference state:

> Today is the day that the Japanese are going to bring their answer to Hull and everything in MAGIC indicated they had been keeping the time back until now in order to accomplish something hanging in the air. Knox and I arranged a conference with Hull at 10:30 and we talked the whole matter over. Hull is very certain that the Japs are planning some deviltry and we are all wondering where the blow will strike.

The 1 p.m. message was delivered to the President about 10:30 a.m.

Why did the high command in Washington fail to disclose promptly to Admiral Kimmel, General Short, and other American commanders in the field the information available in Washington, Saturday night and early Sunday morning? In seeking the answer to this question we have encountered failures of memory and changes in sworn testimony. I am constrained to reach these conclusions.

As a result of his conversation with the President late Saturday night December 6, Admiral Stark, Chief of Naval Operations, did receive notice of a critical turn in Japanese–American relations. Even if it be assumed that he had no inkling until that time of vital information which had been available to him for at least six hours, the call from the President should have provoked his active and immediate efforts to elicit from his subordinates the data which they possessed as to the immediacy of war. He failed to make such efforts.

Sunday morning, when the Saturday messages are known to have come to his attention together with the 1 p.m. message, he again did not take action, despite the recommendations of the Chief of Naval Intelligence that a warning be sent to the fleet. He failed to exercise the care and diligence which his position required.

General Marshall, Chief of Staff of the Army, had the "pilot message" available to him on the afternoon of Saturday, December 6. This placed on him an obligation to make sure he would promptly receive the subsequent information which the pilot message indicated would be soon forthcoming. He did not do so. In placing himself outside of effective contact with his subordinates for several hours on Sunday morning, he failed to exercise the care and diligence which his position required.

The alleged failure of the chief subordinates of Admiral Stark and General Marshall to furnish them promptly with the intercepted messages on Saturday night was unusual for two reasons. First, it was a departure from the usual routine for the distribution of intercepts. Second, these two were the only usual recipients of intercepts who testified that the messages were not brought to their attention on Saturday night. Neither Admiral Stark nor General Marshall made any effort thereafter to ascertain why such a colossal breakdown should occur in the functioning of their staffs on the eve of war.

I have pointed out that during the critical period prior to the attack, the Administration in Washington made certain over-all policy decisions as to how to deal with the Japanese crisis. One decision was that Japan should commit the first overt act against the United States; and thus resolve the dilemma in which the Administration's secret diplomacy had placed it. The other was to be in instant readiness to strike at Japan to check her further aggression against the British and Dutch in Far East Asia. Certainly the information and orders sent to General Short and Admiral Kimmel prior to the attack reflected the policy adopted in Washington.

General Short and Admiral Kimmel were not informed about the most important diplomatic steps in 1941. They were not informed of the parallel action agreement at the Atlantic Conference or the warning to Japan which followed. They were not informed of the significant terms of the American note to Japan of November 26. They were not informed of the commitment made to Great Britain, as set forth in the Brooke-Popham telegram of December 6. They did not receive the vital intercepted Japanese messages or any condensation or summary of them. In response to Admiral Kimmel's request for information in his letter of May 26, 1941, he did receive, in July 1941 from the Navy Department, the actual text of seven intercepted Japanese diplomatic messages.

In the week before the attack he received the text of another intercepted message describing the Japanese intrigue in Thailand. Admiral Kimmel testified that he believed that he was getting all pertinent information affecting the Pacific Fleet. This was the assurance Admiral Stark had given in response to the definite request in the letter of May 26, 1941.

The Intelligence Officer of the Pacific Fleet, Captain Layton, wrote to Captain McCollum, his opposite number in Naval Intelligence in Washington, on March 11, 1941, to urge that intercepted Japanese diplomatic traffic be sent to the fleet. McCollum's reply satisfied Layton that the fleet would receive diplomatic traffic which affected its actions. But the vital intercepts were not sent to Admiral Kimmel or General Short. The fact that a few intercepts were sent to Admiral Kimmel shows that the withholding of others was not attributable to fear of the security of naval communications and consequent prejudice to the secret of "Magic". The "bomb plot" message and related intercepts would have been of incalculable value both to General Short and Admiral Kimmel. Yet they were given no intimation of their existence.

The message of November 27 to Admiral Kimmel warned him of the threatened Japanese move in Southeast Asia and ordered him to be ready to execute a fleet offensive against the Marshalls required by War Plans. Readiness for an offensive at some distance from Hawaii precluded concentrating the limited resources of the fleet upon the defense of its base, which no dispatch from the Navy Department mentioned as a point of attack. The offensive missions prescribed by the War Plans required the full use of the patrol planes of the fleet. These planes were recently acquired and required alterations and maintenance work to put them in shape for war. The planes were too few for full distant searches from Hawaii. Partial searches were properly considered of doubtful value and involved the risk of making the planes useless for the reconnaissance required in the raids on the Marshalls at the time when they would be needed. Task forces at sea and patrol planes going to and from outlying islands carried out such distant reconnaissance as was feasible. As suggested by the Navy Department on November 27, the two carriers of the Pacific Fleet were sent on missions to outlying islands. Lacking air protection the battleships appeared better disposed in port than at sea. The fuel limitations and other logistic deficiencies of the Pacific Fleet were so acute that it was physically impossible to keep the whole fleet, or major portions of it, at sea for extended intervals. The disposition of the ships and the use of patrol planes on and after November 27 were logical and reasonable in view of the message of that date.

On the evening of December 6, in response to Secretary Stimson's request and at the direction of Secretary Knox, the Navy Department compiled from its records a summary showing that all the major ships of the Pacific Fleet were in Pearl Harbor. At this time the information available in Washington showed that war was only hours away. Yet the two Secretaries and the high command made no effort to direct any change in the dispositions of the fleet as shown in the Navy Department summary.

They took no steps to furnish Admiral Kimmel the information which they possessed as to the imminence of war. Consequently they deprived him of any chance to alter his dispositions in the light of that information. I conclude that Secretaries Stimson and Knox and the high command in Washington knew that the major units of the fleet were in Pearl Harbor on December 6–7, 1941, and were satisfied with that situation.

The message of November 27 to Admiral Kimmel illustrates one feature of the pre-Pearl Harbor plan of action of the Administration. The fleet was to be in readiness for offensive raids on the Marshalls to counter the Japanese advance in Southeast Asia. The message sent to General Short by General Marshall on November 27, 1941 shows the other feature of the Administration's plan of action to make sure that the Japanese would strike first so that the offensive by the fleet would be approved by the American public. The message to General Short stated:

> If hostilities cannot, repeat cannot be avoided the United States desires that Japan commit the first overt act. This policy should not, repeat not, be construed as restricting you to a course of action that might jeopardize your

defense. Prior to hostile Japanese action you are directed to undertake such reconnaissance and other measures as you deem necessary but these measures should be carried out so as not, repeat not, to alarm the civil population or disclose intent.

General Marshall testified that instructions about the "overt act" were put into the message on the personal order of the President. In addition the War Department sent three other messages to the Army and Army Air Forces in Hawaii, on November 27 and 28, all of which were directed to sabotage and subversive activities. One of these messages from the War Department on November 28 stated: "Protective measures should be confined to those essential to security, avoiding unnecessary publicity and alarm."

The Navy Department also cautioned Admiral Kimmel against committing the first overt act. On November 29 he received from the Navy Department the substance of the Army's message to General Short with the additional directive: "Undertake no offensive action until Japan has committed an overt act."

On November 27, 1941, General Short reported to General Marshall the measures he had taken in response to General Marshall's message. His reply specifically referred to General Marshall's message by its number. It stated: "Report Department alerted to prevent sabotage, liaison with the Navy. Re your message four seven two twenty-seventh." The Chief of the War Plans Division of the Army, General Leonard T. Gerow, saw General Short's reply, noted and initialed it. This reply was routed by General Gerow to General Marshall, Chief of Staff.

Some question has arisen as to whether General Marshall in fact actually saw General Short's reply. In order that the reader may have the exact facts, I desire to report the evidence, question and answer, beginning page 1,420 of the printed record:

> *Mr Keefe* Now with the country on the brink of war, General Marshall, you having the then impression as you have stated it a few moments ago, that Japan was liable to precipitate war by attacking any time any place, it would be highly important to the Chief of Staff to see to it that the orders which he had given were carried out, would it not?
>
> *General Marshall* That is correct, sir.
>
> *Mr Keefe* Now when General Short's message came back the evidence indicates, somewhat inconclusively perhaps, that it was part of three or four papers, the top one being the reply of MacArthur, then Short, then a route sheet, the MacArthur message being on top and that bears your endorsement with your initials.
>
> *General Marshall* Correct, sir.
>
> *Mr Keefe* Your initials do not appear on the Short message but they do show the initials of the Secretary of War and the War Plans Department, General Gerow. Now am I correct in the assumption from an understanding of your evidence on that point that you think you must have seen the Short message although you did not initial it, having initialed the top one?
>
> *General Marshall* That was my assumption, sir.
>
> *Mr Keefe* Well, is that a mere assumption or is it a fact?
>
> *General Marshall* I stated I did not recall, sir; that I must assume that I had seen it.
>
> *Mr Keefe* Well, if you saw that Short message, General Marshall, as Chief of Staff it imposed some responsibility upon you, did it not?
>
> *General Marshall* That is correct, sir.

Mr Keefe It was addressed to you as Chief of Staff, was it not?

General Marshall That is correct, sir.

Mr Keefe And the very telegram itself indicates that it is in response to the command order which you had issued to him?

General Marshall That is correct, sir.

Mr Keefe And it was a message which attempted on the part of Short to convey to you as Chief of Staff the nature of the alert under which he was operating?

General Marshall That is correct, sir.

Mr Keefe That was his response to your order?

General Marshall Yes, sir.

Mr Keefe Now, I have read the various statements, General Marshall, that you have made at various times in connection with this matter. You recall that when you were before the Army board first you were somewhat confused about those things because you thought that at some time in November there had been a change in alert numbers. Do you remember that?

General Marshall Yes, sir.

Mr Keefe Now, it is perfectly clear now that a reading of this message indicates that there isn't any alert number specified in Short's wire.

General Marshall That is correct, sir.

Mr Keefe So that puts that out of the picture, doesn't it?

General Marshall Yes, sir.

Mr Keefe So we get down to the simple fact that here is a message from your commanding general in the bastion of defense in the Pacific to which all of our defenses, as you have testified, were tied, in which he tells you that he is alerted to prevent sabotage, liaison with Navy. Now in all fairness, General Marshall in the exercise of ordinary care as Chief of Staff, ought you not to have proceeded to investigate further and give further orders to General Short when it appeared that he was only alerted against sabotage?

General Marshall As I stated earlier, that was my opportunity to intervene and I did not do it.

Mr Keefe Well, now, you say that was your opportunity. That was your responsibility, was it not?

General Marshall You can put it that way, sir.

Mr Keefe Well, I don't want to put it that way. I am asking you. You used the words "that was your opportunity," I do not want an opportunity to arise in the future discussion of this matter to have a conflict of words and not to be able to understand just what you meant. Do I understand that your use of the word "opportunity" is synonymous with responsibility?

General Marshall Mr Keefe, I had an immense number of papers going over my desk every day informing me what was happening anywhere in the world. This was a matter of great importance. It had gone into the machine, it had been sent out, the acknowledgments had come back. They passed the important messages over my desk. I noted them and initialed them; those that I thought the Secretary of War ought specifically to see I put them out for him to see, to be sure that he would see it in case by any chance he did not see the same message.

I was not passing the responsibility on to the Secretary of War. I merely wanted him to know.

Now the same thing related to these orders of the War Department. I was responsible. I was responsible for the actions of the General Staff throughout on large matters and on the small matters. I was responsible for those, but I am not a bookkeeping machine and it is extremely difficult, it is an extremely difficult thing for me to take each thing in its turn and give it exactly the attention that it had merited.

Now in this particular case a very tragic thing occurred there is no question about that, there is no question in regard to my responsibility as Chief of Staff. I am not attempting to evade that at all, but I do not think it is quite characterized in the manner that you have expressed yourself.

Mr Keefe Well, now, let me put it in another way. You have now stated it was your responsibility as Chief of Staff to see to it that General Short out there in Hawaii, which you have described as being your bastion of defense, to see that he was alerted, and if he misinterpreted your order to see that that order was carried out.

General Marshall That is my responsibility, sir.

Mr Keefe Now, I have stated it correctly, haven't I?

General Marshall Yes, sir, you have.

Subsequently, in the same examination, General Marshall stated that General Gerow had a direct responsibility in this matter and that he had full responsibility as Chief of Staff.

General Marshall was very fair. He admitted that a tragic mistake had been made, and while it was the direct responsibility of General Gerow, Chief of War Plans, to have "caught" General Short's reply and to have immediately advised his Chief of Staff, yet General Marshall as Chief of Staff did assume over-all responsibility for failure of the Washington headquarters to interpret and evaluate General Short's reply and to see to it that he was on an all-out alert in accordance with the command directive issued in the message from Marshall to Short on November 27.

The Secretary of War saw, noted, and initialed General Short's reply. It was the responsibility of General Marshall to see that General Short was properly alerted. General Short, after being ordered to report his state of readiness to General Marshall, was entitled to assume that this state of readiness was satisfactory to the Chief of Staff unless he heard to the contrary. Neither General Marshall, General Gerow, nor Secretary of War Stimson made any criticism or suggestion to General Short about the condition of his alert in Hawaii in the 10-day period prior to the attack. Because of their silence General Short was led to believe that the Chief of Staff approved his alert against sabotage. I believe that Secretary Stimson, and Generals Marshall and Gerow, understood the nature of his alert which was plainly indicated in the reply itself, I further believe they were satisfied with General Short's alert until the blow fell on Hawaii.

On June 17, 1940, General Marshall had placed the Hawaiian Department on all-out war alert by the following message:

> Immediately alert complete defensive organization to deal with possible trans-Pacific raid comma to greatest extent possible without creating public hysteria or provoking undue curiosity of newspapers or alien agents. Suggest maneuver basis. Maintain alert until further orders. Instructions for secret communication direct with Chief of Staff will be furnished you shortly. Acknowledge.

General Marshall followed up this alert with great care and received considerable detailed information about it. He described the information which caused the alert in 1940 in a letter to the commanding general in Hawaii, General Herron, as follows:

> You have no doubt wondered as to the alert instructions sent to you on the 17th. Briefly, the combination of information from a number of sources led to the

deduction that recent Japanese–Russian agreement to compose their differences in the Far East was arrived at and so timed as to permit Japan to undertake a trans-Pacific raid against Oahu, following the departure of the US Fleet from Hawaii.

Presumably such a raid would be in the interest of Germany and Italy, to force the United States to pull the Fleet back to Hawaii.

Whether the information or deductions were correct, I cannot say. Even if they were, the precautions you have taken may keep us from knowing they were by discouraging any overt act.

On November 27, 1941, the information which General Marshall had showed a far more severe crisis in Japanese–American relations than existed in June of 1940. As his letter to General Herron shows he felt that this all-out alert in Hawaii in 1940 may have discouraged the Japanese from attacking that area. Yet he did not repeat on November 27, 1941, his message of June 17, 1940, to Hawaii with its clear-cut order: "Immediately alert complete defensive organization to deal with possible trans-Pacific raid." He assigned as a reason for not doing so, the fact that in the message of November 27, 1941, "you had to include the instructions of the President regarding overt acts."

Mr Stimson describes the preparation of the Army message of November 27 to General Short as follows:

If there was to be war, moreover, we wanted the Japanese to commit the first overt act. On the other hand, the matter of defense against an attack by Japan is first consideration. In Hawaii because of the large numbers of Japanese habitants, it was felt desirable to issue a special warning so that nothing would be done, unless necessary to defense, to alarm the civil population and thus possibly precipitate an incident and give the Japanese an excuse to go to war and the chance to say that we had committed the first overt act.

Again on December 7, Mr Stimson noted in his diary:

When the news first came that Japan had attacked us, my first feeling was of relief that the indecision was over and that a crisis had come in a way which would unite all our people. This continued to be my dominant feeling in spite of the news of catastrophes which quickly developed.

The same fear of publicity, alarm, or anything which might savor of a first overt act by the United States, rather than by Japan, is reflected in the President's message to High Commissioner Sayre in the Philippines on November 26, 1941. After describing the crisis in Japanese–American relations, the President directed Mr Sayre to impress upon the President of the Philippines "the desirability of avoiding public pronouncement or action since that might make the situation more difficult."

On Saturday night December 6 the President read the first 13 parts of the final Japanese diplomatic note, remarked "This means war," and decided to get in touch with the Chief of Naval Operations. He learned that the Chief of Naval Operations was at the theater. He then stated that he would reach the admiral later, that he did not want to cause public alarm by having the admiral paged. The fact that the admiral had a box reserved was mentioned. The President did not wish him to leave suddenly because he would surely be seen and undue alarm might be caused.

General Marshall failed to use the scrambler telephone on his desk to call General Short in Hawaii on Sunday morning December 7, nearly two hours before the attack, and give him the same information which he sent in the delayed telegram which reached General Short after the attack.

General Marshall testified that among the possible factors which may have influenced him against using the scrambler telephone was the possibility that the Japanese could construe the fact that the Army was alerting its garrisons in Hawaii as a hostile act.

> The Japanese would have grasped at most any straw to bring to such portions of our public that doubted our integrity of action that we were committing an act that forced action on their part.

The concept of an "incident" as a factor which would unify public opinion behind an all-out war effort either in the Atlantic or Pacific had influenced the thinking of officials in Washington for a long time. Many plans which might have produced an incident were from time to time discussed and considered. As early as October 10, 1940 Secretary Knox had advised Admiral Richardson, then Commander in Chief of the Pacific Fleet, of a plan the President was considering to shut off all trade between Japan and North and South America. This would be accomplished by means of a patrol of American ships in two lines extending from Hawaii westward to the Philippines, and from Samoa toward the Dutch East Indies. This plan was to be instituted in the event Japan retaliated against Great Britain upon the reopening of the Burma Road scheduled for October 17, 1940. Admiral Richardson was amazed at this proposal and stated that the fleet was not prepared to put such a plan into effect, nor for the war which would certainly result from such a course of action.

On February 11, 1941, the Chief of Naval Operations in a memorandum for the President, described the

President as considering a plan to send a detachment of vessels to the Far East and perhaps to permit a "leak" that they were going out there. He quoted the President in the same memorandum as stating that he would not mind losing one or two cruisers, but that he did not want to take a chance on losing five or six. Again, in a letter of April 19, 1941, the Chief of Naval Operations quoted the President as saying to him:

> Betty, just as soon as those ships come back from Australia and New Zealand, or perhaps a little before, I want to send some more out. I just want to keep them popping up here and there and keep the Japs guessing.

On May 24, 1941, Admiral Stark wrote Admiral Kimmel: "Day before yesterday the President gave me an overall limit of 30 days to prepare and have ready an expedition of 25,000 men to sail for and to take the Azores. Whether or not there would be opposition I do not know but we have to be fully prepared for strenuous opposition."

On July 25, 1941 the Chief of Naval Operations wrote Admiral Kimmel to the effect that he might be called upon to send a carrier-load of planes to Russia via one of the Asiatic Russian ports. "I don't know that you will, but the President has told me to be prepared for it, and I want you to have the thought." Admiral Kimmel replied to this suggestion as follows:

> I entertain no doubt that such an operation, if discovered (as is highly probable), will be tantamount to initiation of a Japanese–American war. If we are going to take the initiative in commencing such a war, I can think of more effective ways for gaining initial advantage. In short, it is my earnest conviction that use of a carrier to deliver aircraft to Asiatic Russian ports in the present period of

strained relations is to invite war. If we have decided upon
war it would be far better to take direct offensive action. If
for reasons of political expediency, it has been determined
to force Japan to fire the first shot, let us choose a method
which will be more advantageous to ourselves.

On July 31, 1941, Admiral Stark sent Admiral Kimmel a
copy of a letter to Captain Charles M. Cooke as follows:

Within 48 hours after the Russian situation broke I went
to the President, with the Secretary's approval, and stated
that on the assumption that the country's decision is not to
let England fall, we should immediately seize the
psychological opportunity presented by the
Russian–German clash and announce and start escorting
immediately and protecting the Western Atlantic on a large
scale; that such a declaration, followed by immediate action
on our part, would almost certainly involve us in the war
and that I considered every day of delay in our getting into
the war as dangerous and that much more delay might be
fatal to Britain's survival. I reminded him that I had been
asking this for months in the State Department and
elsewhere, etc., etc., etc.

I have been maintaining that only a war psychology
could or would speed things up the way they should be
speeded up, that strive as we would it just is not in the
nature of things to get the results in peace that we would,
were we at war.

The Iceland situation may produce an "incident." You
are as familiar with that and the President's statements and
answers at press conferences as I am. Whether or not we
will get an "incident" because of the protection we are
giving Iceland and the shipping which we must send in
support of Iceland and our troops, I do not know. Only
Hitler can answer.

Again Admiral Kelly Turner, War Plans Officer for the Chief of Naval Operations stated, in describing United States–British Staff conversations on War Plans in 1941:

> It was felt by the Naval Department that there might be a possibility of war with Japan without the involvement of Germany, but at some length and over a considerable period this matter was discussed and it was determined that in such a case the United States would, if possible, initiate "efforts to bring Germany into the war against us in order that we would be able to give strong support to the United Kingdom in Europe."

On November 29, 1941, the Chief of Naval Operations sent a dispatch to the Commander in Chief of the Asiatic Fleet which commenced with this unusual statement:

> President directs that the following be done as soon as possible and within two days if possible after receipt this dispatch.

The President's directions were that the Commander in Chief of the Asiatic Fleet was to charter three small vessels to form a "defensive information patrol." The minimum requirements to establish these ships as United States men-of-war would suffice in manning them. These requirements were: command by a naval officer and the mounting of a small gun and one machine gun. The employment of Filipino crews with the minimum number naval ratings was authorized. The ships were to observe and report by radio Japanese movement in the West China Sea and Gulf of Siam. The President prescribed the point at which each vessel was to be stationed. One vessel was to be stationed between Hainan and Hue; one between Camranh Bay and Cape St Jaques; one off Pointe De Camau.

All these points were clearly in the path of the Japanese advance down the coast of Indo-China, and toward the Gulf of Siam. The Navy Department did not originate this plan. The Navy Department would not have directed it to be done unless the President had specifically ordered it. Admiral Hart was already conducting reconnaissance off that coast by planes from Manila. So far as the Navy Department was concerned, sufficient information was being received from this air reconnaissance.

Had the Japanese fired upon anyone of these three small vessels, it would have constituted an overt act on the part of Japan.

AFTERMATH OF THE PEARL HARBOR ATTACK

Eleven days after Pearl Harbor, the Roberts Commission was appointed by the President to find the facts about the Pearl Harbor attack. Its duty was:

> to provide bases for sound decisions whether any derelictions of duty or errors of judgment on the part of United States Army or Navy personnel contributed to such successes as were achieved by the enemy, and, if so, what these derelictions or errors were, and who were responsible therefor.

General Marshall and Admiral Stark were witnesses at the first meeting of the Commission. Their testimony was not given under oath and was not recorded. Neither was that of their chief subordinates, Admiral Turner and General Gerow. The Commission examined General Short and Admiral Kimmel under oath in Hawaii. They were not

permitted to be present during the testimony of other witnesses, to examine or cross-examine them, or to know
what evidence had been presented.

The Commission knew that Japanese messages had
been intercepted and were available, prior to the attack, to
the high command in Washington. It did not inquire about
what information these intercepts contained or who
received them.

Mr Justice Roberts testified before this Committee: "I
would not have bothered to read it (the intercepted
Japanese traffic) if it had been shown to us." Misleading
statements made to the Roberts Commission by high
ranking naval officers in Washington to the effect that
Admiral Kimmel had all the information available to the
Navy Department went unchallenged.

The Roberts Commission's failure to inquire into the
Japanese intercepts and their distribution and evaluation in
Washington, prevented it from correctly assessing responsibility for the disaster. The facts were then fresh in the
minds of key witnesses in Washington. They could not
then have honestly forgotten their whereabouts at important times. When the Roberts Commission bypassed the
facts about the intercepted messages, it nearly buried the
truth about Pearl Harbor. Its report became the indictment
of two officers based upon incomplete evidence.

The Roberts report was published on January 25,
1942. General Short, reading it in the press, was dumb-
founded and immediately called his friend General
Marshall on the telephone to inquire whether he should
retire. Marshall advised him to "stand pat," but told Short
he would consider the telephone conversation "authority"
for Short's retirement if it became necessary. On the same
day, the Secretary of the Navy directed that Admiral
Kimmel in San Francisco be informed that Short had sub-

mitted a request for retirement. This information was immediately telephoned to Kimmel. Kimmel, who had not previously thought of retiring, construed the telephone message as a request that he do so and submitted a formal request for retirement dated January 26, 1942. General Short, who thought it was not fair to General Marshall to have to act only on the basis of a telephone conversation, sent to Marshall a formal request for retirement in writing, addressed to the Adjutant General dated January 25, 1942.

On January 26 General Marshall recommended to Secretary of War Stimson that General Short's application for retirement be accepted "today" but that it be done "quietly without any publicity at the moment."

Admiral Stark requested the Army to keep him advised about Short's retirement as he proposed to "communicate this fact to Admiral Kimmel in the hope Kimmel will likewise apply for retirement." However, on January 28, 1942, he sent a telephone message to Kimmel to the effect that the previous telephone notification about Short's retirement was not intended to influence him. Thereupon Admiral Kimmel submitted his letter of January 28, 1942, to the Secretary of the Navy, in which he stated: "I desire my request for retirement to stand, subject only to determination by the Department as to what course of action will best serve the interests of the country and the good of the service."

The President personally directed the method of handling the requests for the retirement of Kimmel and Short. On January 29, 1942, he instituted a three-point program for dealing with the matter.

The Army and Navy were to act together. After a week's waiting they were to announce that Kimmel and Short had applied for the retirement and that their applications were under consideration. After another week had passed, public announcement was to be made that the applications had been accepted with the condition that acceptance did not bar subsequent court-martial proceedings. Court-martial proceedings, however, were to be described as impossible without the disclosure of military secrets. The wording of the condition in the acceptance was troublesome to the Administration.

The President, Secretary Stimson, Secretary Knox, and Attorney General Biddle labored over the language. The Administration wanted to avoid public criticism for having barred court-martial proceedings. On the other hand, it did not wish to stimulate the public or the two officers to expect or demand court-martial proceedings. Finally language as suitable as possible was agreed upon. The phrase to be used in accepting the retirement applications was "without condonation of any offense or prejudice to future disciplinary action." Admiral Kimmel and General Short were each retired by letters so worded, dated respectively, February 16 and February 17, 1942. The Secretary of the Navy, in announcing the Navy's action, stated that he had directed the preparation of charges for court martial of Admiral Kimmel alleging dereliction of duty. The public were informed that a trial could not be held until such time as the public interest and safety would permit.

The public reaction was as planned. Kimmel and Short were considered solely responsible for Pearl Harbor. The Roberts report considered by Justice Roberts as only an indictment, became, in effect, a conviction.

The two officers were helpless. No court martial could be had. They had no way of defending themselves. They remained in ignorance of what evidence the Roberts Commission had heard. Admiral Stark wrote to Admiral Kimmel on February 21, 1942:

Pending something definite, there is no reason why you should not settle yourself in a quiet nook somewhere and let Old Father Time help the entire situation which I feel he will if for no other reason than he always has.

The high civilian and military officials in Washington who had skillfully maneuvered Kimmel and Short into the position of exclusive blame knew at the time all the hidden facts about Pearl Harbor, at least as much and probably more than this investigation has been able to uncover. As the two-year statutory period for instituting court-martial proceedings was about to expire, Kimmel and Short were requested by the Secretaries of War and Navy to waive the Statute of Limitations. Admiral Kimmel did so but with the provision that any court martial be held in "open court." General Short did likewise.

Similar requests were not made of other officers, not even of those who before this Committee publicly accepted responsibility for certain failures of the high command in Washington.

In June of 1944 the Congress directed the Secretaries of War and Navy to conduct investigations into the Pearl Harbor attack. The War Department denied the Army Board of Investigation access to the intercepted messages. General Miles, Director of Military Intelligence, at the time of Pearl Harbor, was ordered by General Marshall not to testify on the subject of the intercepts. For a considerable period the Navy Court of Inquiry was denied access to the same material.

After repeated demands by Admiral Kimmel, the Navy Department released this restriction upon its own Court. The War Department finally followed the same course. For the first time, late in the Board's proceedings, Army officers were permitted to testify before the Army Board as to all details regarding the intercepts. But many important

Army witnesses had already testified under the limitations previously ordered.

In the fall of 1944 the Army Board and Navy Court made their reports to the Secretaries of the War and Navy. These reports were critical of the conduct of Admiral Stark and General Marshall. The findings were not made public. The Navy Court exonerated Admiral Kimmel. Admiral Kimmel's request to read its report was refused by the Secretary of the Navy. The Secretaries of War and Navy instituted further secret investigations dispensing with the services of the three-man Board and Court previously established, and each entrusting the conduct of proceedings to a single officer.

Admiral Kimmel's request to be present at the further Navy investigation, to introduce evidence, to confront and cross-examine witnesses, was denied by the Secretary of the Navy. The affidavits and testimony at the further investigations contain many instances where witnesses gave evidence materially different from that which they had previously sworn to before the Army Board and the Naval Court. These changes were especially marked in testimony of certain key witnesses on the subject of the dissemination and evaluation of the intercepted messages in Washington. Again, before this Committee these same witnesses further changed their testimony from that sworn to twice previously, or pleaded lapses of memory.

The record of the high military and civilian officials of the War and Navy Departments in dealing with the Pearl Harbor disaster from beginning to end does them no credit. It will have a permanent bad effect on the morale and integrity of the armed services. The Administration had ample opportunity to record and preserve all the acts about Pearl Harbor, even if their public disclosure needed to wait upon the war's end. This was not done. The policy adopted was to place the public responsibility for the disaster on the commanders in the field, to be left there for all time. The policy failed only because suppression created public suspicion, and the Congress was alert.

CONCLUSIONS AND RECOMMENDATIONS

This investigation has not brought to light all the facts about Pearl Harbor. We have been denied much vital information. Mr Stimson did not answer certain important interrogations which, in consideration of the state of his health, were submitted to him in writing. He has also denied to the Committee his diary entries for the days December 2 to December 6, 1941. These were significantly omitted from his written statement.

Mr Hull's health permitted only a brief appearance before us and no examination by the minority members of the Committee. Written interrogatories were submitted as to when he first saw or obtained information as to the contents of certain vital intercepted messages, including the 1 p.m. message. Mr Hull answered: "I do not recall the exact times that I first saw or learned of the contents of the messages you cite." "I do not recall" was an answer frequently received from other important witnesses. Messrs Maxwell Hamilton, Eugene Dooman and Stanley Hornbeck, State Department officials who played important roles in 1941 in our Far Eastern diplomacy, have not testified. We have been denied Ambassador Grew's diary. In December 1941 General Bedell Smith was secretary to the General Staff of the Army. He did not testify. His possible knowledge of the distribution of intercepted messages to General Marshall on Saturday evening, December 6, was not investigated. Admiral (then Captain) Glover was the duty officer in the office of the Chief of Naval Operations on December 6, 1941. His log for that night contained the vital information about Mr Stimson's interest in precise locations of the ships of the Pacific Fleet. Admiral Glover sent the Committee a telegram but did not testify. Mr Welles' memoranda of Atlantic Charter conferences was obtained from the State Department only after his oral testimony before us had been completed.

On the evidence before us I concur in the findings of the Committee with respect to responsibilities of our commanders in Hawaii. I believe that the "mistakes of judgment" referred to in the committee report are directly related to the failures of the high commands in Washington to have their organizations fully alerted and on a war footing and that those in command at the Washington level must bear their full share of the responsibility for the tragedy of Pearl Harbor.

I further conclude that secret diplomacy was at the root of the tragedy.

The United States had warned Japan that an advance to Malaya or the Dutch East Indies would mean war with this nation. The President gave Great Britain assurances of our armed support in such an event. What Japan and Britain knew, our commanders in the field and our own people did not know. Washington feared that national unity could not be attained unless Japan committed the first overt act. Accordingly, the Army in Hawaii was put on an anti-sabotage alert, a defensive posture containing the least possible risk of incident in Hawaii which Japan might claim was an overt act by the United States. The mobilization of American public opinion in support of an offensive by the Pacific Fleet against Japan was to be accomplished, if at all, by a message to Congress "at the last stage of our relations, relating to actual hostilities." This message was to be the prelude to hostilities by the United States if Japan attacked the British and the Dutch at the outset of the war and did not attack this nation. A direct attack by Japan against the United States at the outset of hostilities would make such a message unnecessary.

Mr Stimson's diary describes the plan succinctly: "The question was how we should maneuver them into the position of firing the first shot without allowing too much danger to ourselves." In formulating this plan undoubtedly Washington was influenced by public promises to keep us out of war unless attacked.

With full knowledge of Japan's intentions prior to the attack, Washington had one plain duty to the American people. That duty was to inform them of their peril. This was not done. Washington had a further duty to make sure that our forces were ready to meet the attack by furnishing their commanders afield and afloat with all available information, or by evaluating that information and giving them appropriate clear and categoric instructions.

Those who find in various instances of poor coordination between the services the causes of Pearl Harbor are satisfied with a superficial explanation. The state of readiness of our armed forces in the field was a refection of over-all policy adopted on the highest level in Washington. The President had delivered to him the Japanese intercepted messages and possessed much more information about Japanese plans and intentions than any field commander. He gave most minute directions to commanders in the field, even as to the scouting positions of individual ships, when he thought such directions necessary. A merger of the armed forces and unity of command in Hawaii in November and December, 1941, could not have eliminated the dangers in the policy of maneuvering Japan into striking the first blow. That policy would still have shaped the orders given, as well as the information sent to a single commander in the field.

Those who find American public opinion responsible for Pearl Harbor accept an entirely false theory.

Enlightened public opinion is based on accurate public information. The American people, if kept well informed of their real diplomatic position, do not need an incident to unite them. If foreign policy and diplomatic representations are treated as the exclusive, secret information of the President and his advisers, public opinion will not be enlightened. The very nature of the consequent public alarm places the armed forces of the Nation in effective readiness and may even deter an enemy from executing its planned attack. The best deterrent to a predatory Japan in late 1941 was a thoroughly informed and obviously alerted America.

In this connection it will be noted that when the reports of the Army Board and the Navy Court of Inquiry were submitted to President Truman on August 30, 1945, he made the following statement:

> I have read it (the Pearl Harbor reports) very carefully, and I came to the conclusion that the whole thing is the result of the policy which the country itself pursued. The country was not ready for preparedness. Every time the President made an effort to get a preparedness program through the Congress, it was stifled. Whenever the President made a statement about the necessity of preparedness he was vilified for doing it. I think the country is as much to blame as any individual in this final situation that developed in Pearl Harbor.

An examination of the facts ought to compel any person to reject this conclusion. The record clearly demonstrates how the Army and Navy get the funds needed for national defense. The Army and Navy are required to submit their respective estimates each year to the Bureau of the Budget.

This Bureau acting for the President conducts hearings and finally makes recommendations to the President as to the amounts to be recommended to the Congress for appropriation. The Congress is in effect the people of America. The record discloses that in the fiscal years 1934 to 1941, inclusive, the Army and Navy jointly asked for $26,580,145,930. This is the combined total of Army and Navy requests made to the Bureau of the Budget. In the same period the President recommended to the Congress that it appropriate to the combined services $23,818,319,897. The Congress actually made available to the Army and Navy in this period $24,943,987,823. Thus it is apparent that the President himself recommended to the Congress in the fiscal years 1934 to 1941, inclusive, that it appropriate for the Army and Navy $2,761,826,033 less than had been requested by the Army and Navy. The people's representatives in the Congress gave to the Army and Navy in the form of appropriations and authorizations for expenditure $1,256,667,926 more than the President had recommended in his budget messages to the Congress.

The mere recital of these undisputed figures should dispose of the contention that "the country is as much to blame as any individual in this final situation that developed in Pearl Harbor." I am including herein for ready reference a complete statement:

	Asked ($)	Budget ($)	Congress ($)
1934	320,900,513	280,746,841	280,066,381
1935	305,271,321	288,960,155	283,862,094
1936	361,351,154	331,799,277	363,224,957
1937	467,022,915	391,065,510	401,914,645
1938	468,204,851	436,495,336	439,872,423
1939	630,803,130	598,016,016	611,848,391
1940	1,019,342,730	995,442,760	970,822,098
1941	13,612,977,763	13,067,553,812	13,487,184,058
Total	17,185,874,377	16,390,079,707	16,828,795,047

	Asked ($)	Budget ($)	Congress ($)
Total both services	17,185,874,377 9,394,271,553	6,390,079,707 7,428,240,190	16,828,795,047 8,115,192,776
Total	26,580,145,930	23,818,319,897	24,943,987,823

Roosevelt cut: $2,761,826,033
Congress restored: $1,256,667,926 of the Budget cut

Another subject that has been bandied about the country for a number of years relates to what has been frequently referred to as the failure or refusal of Congress to fortify the island of Guam. The contention has been made that Congress refused to appropriate money to fortify the island of Guam and that as a result of such failure the entire war in the Pacific in its initial stages was lost to the Japanese.

The fact is that no proposal was ever submitted to the Congress involving the fortification of Guam. The Navy did request an appropriation of five million dollars for the purpose of dredging the harbor at Guam. The first request of the Navy was rejected by the Congress. Thereafter, the appropriation requested by the Navy was passed with only one vote against it. The dredging operation was being carried on when war broke out with Japan.

It is interesting to note that "Rainbow No. 5," which is the Joint Chiefs' of Staff worldwide war plan, placed the island of Guam in Category "F."

The following questions and answers tell the story:

Mr Keefe Now, I would like to ask a question which bothered me with respect to your Rainbow No. 5, which places the island of Guam in what is called Category F.

Admiral Stark I have the category here.

Mr Keefe Now will you state for the record what Category F means?

Admiral Stark Yes, sir. We have that, I am sure. This is out of Joint Action, Army and Navy, and refers to degrees of preparation, and they are put in categories of defense, A, B, C, D, E, and F.

Mr Keefe Well, take Guam to start with. That is in F. Now give us what Category F means.

Admiral Stark Category F: "Positions beyond the continental limits of the United States which may be subject to either minor or major attack for the purpose of occupation but which cannot be provided with adequate defense forces. Under this category the employment of existing local forces and local facilities will be confined principally to the demolition of those things it is desirable to prevent falling into the hands of the enemy."

Mr Keefe Then, so far as Guam was concerned, at the time this basic war plan was devised it was the considered opinion of both the Army and Navy that it could not be defended and it therefore was placed in Category F that required those on the island, through demolition or otherwise, to destroy anything of value to the enemy and to permit it to be taken?

Admiral Stark Yes, sir.

Mr Keefe And to surrender?

Admiral Stark Yes, sir.

Mr Keefe That is right, is it not?

Admiral Stark That is correct, yes, sir.

Mr Keefe Now, at the time of the attack on Guam and the capture of Guam by the Japs, were improvements on the harbor being made at that time or had they been completed?

Admiral Stark They had not been completed. Of course, I recall very clearly the legislation with regard to that. I do not know just what their status was at this moment. I had obtained from Congress the appropriation, I believe it was $6,000,000, for certain improvements to the harbor. You recall the first year lost it by six votes, and the following year it went through almost unanimously, by one vote being opposed to it. Just how far we had gotten along with that I do not recall at the moment.

Mr Keefe With those improvements completed, Guam would still be in category F, would it not?

Admiral Stark In the same category, Category F. The improvements were not such as improved the defense of Guam but very little.

Mr Keefe Even with the improvements that were requested and contemplated, the Island of Guam, in the opinion of the Joint Army and Navy Board, could not be successfully defended due to the power that Japan had in the mandated islands surrounding it, is that right?

Admiral Stark That is correct.

These simple facts as disclosed to the public for the first time in these hearings should effectively dispose of the contention that "Congress refused to fortify the Island of Guam, and hence the United States suffered tremendous loss in the initial stages of the war with Japan." In the future the people and their Congress must know how close American diplomacy is moving to war so that they may check its advance if imprudent and support its position if sound. A diplomacy which relies upon the enemy's first overt act to insure effective popular support for the nation's final war decision is both outmoded and dangerous in the atomic age. To prevent any future Pearl Harbor more tragic and damaging than that of December 7, 1941, there must be constant close coordination between American public opinion and American diplomacy.

THE MINORITY PEARL HARBOR REPORT

We, the undersigned, find it impossible to concur with the findings and conclusions of the Committee's report because they are illogical, and unsupported by the preponderance of the evidence before the Committee. The conclusions of the diplomatic aspects are based upon incomplete evidence.

We, therefore, find it necessary to file a report setting forth the conclusions which we believe are properly sustained by evidence before the Committee.

Homer Ferguson
Owen Brewster

THE DUTY OF THE COMMITTEE

The duty of this Committee is fixed by the terms of the joint resolution under which it was created, as expounded by Senator Barkley, author of the resolution, in his address to the Senate on September 6, 1945, explaining the purpose of the resolution.

Section 2 of the joint resolution reads:

> The Committee shall make a full and complete investigation of the facts relating to the events and circumstances leading up to or following the attack made by Japanese armed forces upon Pearl Harbor in the Territory of Hawaii on December 7, 1941, and shall report to the Senate and the House of Representatives not later than January 3, 1946 (later extended to July 16, 1946), the results of its investigation, together with such recommendations as it may seem advisable.

In his address to the Senate on September 6, 1945, Senator Barkley pointed out the need for this investigation by declaring that the reports on Pearl Harbor by the President's Pearl Harbor Commission, the Roberts Commission, the Army Pearl Harbor Board, the Navy Court of Inquiry, and other authorities "are confusing and conflicting, when compared to one another, and to some extent contain contradictions and inconsistencies within themselves." In this connection he referred to the "widespread confusion and suspicion" that prevailed "among the American people and among the Members of Congress."

In all these reports, which had resulted in contradictions, confusion, and inconsistencies, the central issue had been the fixing of responsibility for the catastrophe that befell the American forces at Pearl Harbor on December 7, 1941. This fact Senator Barkley fully recognized in his statement that the first purpose of the investigation is that of "fixing responsibility" for the Pearl Harbor disaster "upon an individual, or a group of individuals, or upon a system under which they operated or cooperated or failed to do either." In fulfilment of this obligation, Senator Barkley said, the investigation:

> should be conducted without partisanship or favoritism toward any responsible official, military, naval, or civilian, high or low, living or dead. Congress itself should make its own thorough, impartial, and fearless inquiry into the facts and circumstances and conditions prevailing prior to and at the time of the Pearl Harbor attack, no matter how far back it may be necessary to go in order to appraise the situation which existed prior to and at the time of the attack.

The Joint Committee, therefore, is charged with the duty of investigating the entire subject de novo. It is and should be free from the findings and conclusions of all previous investigations and inquiries except such material as members of this Committee in their discretion may see fit to cite or incorporate in their report.

The second purpose of the investigation, Senator Barkley explained, is that of ascertaining whether in view of what happened at Pearl Harbor the findings might be useful to Congress in legislating with regard to military and naval forces and the executive departments having control of them, or which are supposed to work with them.

These views of the obligation of the Committee were supported wholeheartedly on the floor of the Senate by Senator Brewster and Senator Ferguson and thereafter the Senate unanimously passed the resolution as so interpreted.

Of necessity, as used in relation to the obligation of this Committee, responsibility means responsibility for failure on the part of individual officers or groups of officers or civilian officials to do their full official duty in preparing for and meeting effectively the Japanese attack on Pearl Harbor on December 7, 1941; and the term "duty" means duty according to the Constitution, laws, and established administrative practices under which all such individuals and groups of individuals were bound to operate prior to and on the day of that catastrophe.

FUNDAMENTAL QUESTIONS BEFORE THE JOINT COMMITTEE

Inasmuch as all decisions and activities connected with this occurrence at Pearl Harbor were decisions and activities of executive authorities of the Government of the United States, the issue of responsibility for the degree of success attained by the Japanese attack involves at least one general question and four subsidiary and specific questions.

The general question is: Did all the civil, military, and naval authorities of the United States charged with responsibility for the conduct of diplomatic negotiations with the Japanese Government and for preparedness and defense at Pearl Harbor competently, efficiently, and with proper regard for the trust imposed in them fulfill the duties of their respective offices under the Constitution and laws of the United States?

The subsidiary and specific questions are:

1. Did the high civil, military, and naval authorities in Washington secure in advance of 10 o'clock a.m. (EST) December 7, 1941, information respecting Japanese designs and intentions sufficient to convince them beyond all reasonable doubt that war with Japan was immediately imminent?
2. If so, did they give to General Walter C. Short and Admiral Husband E. Kimmel, the commanders at

Pearl Harbor, clear and definite orders, immediately prior to the Japanese attack, instructing them to be fully alert for defense against such an attack?

3. Was Hawaii adequately equipped for its defense against a Japanese attack in accordance with the known circumstances?

4. Did the commanders at Pearl Harbor take the appropriate measures required by the orders issued to them from Washington, by the duties of their respective offices, and by the information in their possession and the resources at their disposal, to maintain the security of the possessions of the United States as far as that responsibility was invested in them?

The question of the wisdom of the foreign policy pursued by the Government of the United States is excluded by the terms of the Committee's instructions. In any case, to go into this issue would involve the Committee in the complexities of history extending back more than 50 years and in matters of opinion which cannot be settled by reference to anything as positive and definite as the Constitution, laws, and established administrative practices of the United States Government.

To understand the questions involved, however, an examination of our relations in the Far East, and of the diplomatic negotiations leading up to December 7, 1941, are part and parcel of the explanation of the responsibilities involved in this inquiry.

DIFFICULTIES FACING THE JOINT COMMITTEE AND INCOMPLETENESS OF THE RECORD

When all the testimony, papers, documents, exhibits, and other evidence duly laid before the Committee are reviewed, it becomes apparent that the record is far from complete. The Committee did not have an opportunity to cross-examine any of the high civil executive principals in the Pearl Harbor affair. President Roosevelt and Secretary Knox had died before the Committee was created. Harry Hopkins, who was intimately and officially associated with President Roosevelt, died shortly after the Committee began its work. The health of Secretary of War Stimson and Secretary of State Hull prevented the Committee from getting the full benefit of their knowledge, except for the information they voluntarily furnished.

It is extremely unfortunate that the Roberts Commission Report was so hasty, inconclusive, and incomplete. Some witnesses were examined under oath; others were not. Much testimony was not even recorded. The Commission knew that Japanese messages had been intercepted and were available, prior to the attack, to the high command in Washington. The Commission did not inquire about what information these intercepts contained, who received them, or what was done about them, although the failure of Washington to inform the commanders in Hawaii of this vital intelligence bears directly on the question of whether those commanders performed their full duties. Mr Justice Roberts testified before this Committee:

> I would not have bothered to read it (the intercepted Japanese traffic) if it had been shown to us.

If it were necessary to do so, detailed examples of the many shortcomings of the Roberts Commission could be set forth. The duty of our Committee to examine the entire subject afresh does not require an extended criticism of the Roberts Commission Report.

It should be noted, however, that Justice Roberts had sufficient legal experience to know the proper method of collecting and preserving evidence which in this case involved the highest interests of the Nation. The facts were then fresh in the minds of key witnesses in Washington. They could not then have been ignorant of their where-abouts at important times or have forgotten the details of events and operations. No files would have been "lost" and no information would have been distorted by the passage of time. The failure to observe these obvious necessities is almost as tragic to the cause of truth as the attack on Pearl Harbor itself was a tragedy for the Nation.

These difficulties were supplemented by even greater ones stemming from Presidential restraints on the Committee and from the partisan character of the Committee itself.

Even before the Committee commenced its work, it was confronted with an order issued on August 28, 1945, and signed by President Truman, which severely limited the power of the Committee to gain access to the full facts. The order is as follows:

AUGUST 28, 1945
Memorandum for—The Secretary of State
    The Secretary of War
    The Secretary of the Navy
    The Attorney General
    The Joint Chiefs of Staff
    The Director of the Budget
    The Director of the Office of War Information

Appropriate departments of the Government and the Joint Chiefs of Staff are hereby directed to take such steps as are necessary to prevent release to the public, except with the specific approval of the President in each case, of:

Information regarding the past or present status, technique or procedures, degree of success attained, or any specific results of any crypto-analytic unit acting under the authority of the United States Government or any Department thereof

Harry S. Truman
Restricted.

It was not until October 23, 1945, that President Truman made the order less stringent by a new order. The modification left much to be desired.

The application of the new order was limited to the State, War, and Navy Departments. It relaxed the secrecy of records only so far as "the Joint Committee" was concerned, while it continued to prevent "individual" members of the Committee from searching records as responsible Members of Congress either alone, in groups, or even when accompanied by Committee counsel. By one way or another, control over papers, records, and other information remained in the hands of the majority party members.

The President's October order also contained the unfortunate phrase "any information in their possession material to the investigation," which provided a cloak for those reluctant to yield information requested by members of the Committee. It was always possible to confront individual members with the view that the papers, data, and information desired was not "material to the investigation." Decisions were made by the majority ruling out evidence as "not material to the investigation" without members of the Committee ever seeing the material about which the decision was made.

No subsequent modifying orders wholly removed these restrictions. In an order of November 7, 1945, President Truman relaxed restraints on executives of the Government in order that they may speak freely to individual members of the Committee, but the order closed with the direction: "This does not include any files or written material."

In this fashion every facility and concession afforded to members of the Joint Committee was hedged about with troublesome qualifications and restraints. The relaxation of restraints was often publicized while the continuing qualifications were but little discussed. The effect was to restrict individual members of the Committee in practice while the appearance of their freedom of operations was held out to the public. In justice to Committee counsel and to individual majority members of the Committee, efforts made by them to overcome these restrictions should be recognized. It is a great tribute to their fairness that the Committee did not break up over this issue but continued to work despite the handicaps which were never wholly removed.

The plain fact that an investigation could not be an investigation if Committee members remained mere spectators, persuaded some members that restraints on their freedom were not justified. The flimsiness of the argument for restrictions became even more evident when permission to search files and other records was denied by majority vote to individual members even when accompanied by Committee counsel. Rightly or wrongly it was inferred from this that there was a deliberate design to block the search for the truth.

Such a view was supported by the knowledge that restrictions on individual members of congressional investigatory bodies were contrary to the best practices in other investigations. Some celebrated instances were recalled.

Speaking in the Senate on November 9, 1945, during one of the discussions on Committee powers, the Senator from Montana (Mr Burton K. Wheeler) observed:

I concur in what the Senator from Illinois has said with reference to the authorizing of a single member of the committee to hold hearings. I have served on a good many investigations since I have been a Member of the Senate, and some very important ones. I assisted to quite an extent in the Teapot Dome investigation carried on by my colleague, Senator Walsh, of Montana, and likewise I carried on the investigation of the Department of Justice. I was a minority member of the committee.

In all my experience with any investigating committee, I have never known of any one member of a committee not being permitted to go and look over the files in any department of the Government of the United States. This is the first time I have every known anything of that kind being questioned.

I call attention to the fact that in the Daugherty investigation I sent for files myself, I asked for files from the Attorney General of the United States, Mr Daugherty. He refused to give them to me. I have forgotten the ground he stated, but at any rate he refused to give them to me. When he did so, the President of the United States, Mr Coolidge, called him in and asked for his resignation, and Mr Daugherty was eliminated from the office of Attorney General. After that time, when the new Attorney General was appointed, every single file I ever asked for, as a minority member of the committee, was furnished to me.

As I have stated, my colleague, Senator Walsh, of Montana, was a minority member of the committee investigating the Teapot Dome situation. I know of my own personal knowledge that he got from the Department, and from officials in the Department, information which he afterward used, and if he had not been permitted to do that, and if I had not been permitted to do it, I am sure there would have been a complete failure of the investigation of the Department of Justice.

Another instance is the more recent one in which President Truman himself is well versed. As Senator, Mr Truman headed a distinguished committee bearing the popular designation "The Truman Committee" (now the Mead Committee). The cardinal principle of the Truman Committee in the four years during which it won the respect and confidence of the American people, rested on the proposition that every individual member of the committee was wholly free to search for any information deemed by him to be relevant wherever and whenever he thought it could be found. Never once did the chairman or the majority of the committee refuse to recognize that right and that responsibility of each individual member.

Untrammeled freedom of individual committee members in these instances did not produce chaos or disorder as was argued would be the case in the Pearl Harbor inquiry. On the contrary, the procedure and results in each case did honor to the committees concerned and proved salutary for the Nation. Complete concurrence with the most admirable outline of the purposes and scope of the investigation of the events leading up to Pearl Harbor, and our entry into the World War, as presented to the Senate by the author of the resolution at the time of its introduction, and hearty approval of much that has been done by the Committee, must not blind us to the extent to which the investigation lived up to its advance billing by its distinguished sponsor.

At the very inception the tested practices in investigations of this character that had demonstrated such extraordinary success in the entire history of the Truman Committee were very definitely rejected, and neither of the two members of the Committee who had received rather extended training under the then Senator Truman were allowed to follow the course in the investigation of Pearl Harbor that had repeatedly produced most gratifying results in their earlier experience.

This firm refusal by the Committee majority, consisting of six Democrats as against four Republicans, at the very outset to allow the scope to individual members even with every safeguard proposed against the alleged danger of abuse was both unfortunate and disquieting.

Everything that has since developed must be viewed in the light of this iron curtain that was thus imposed.

Permission was asked to conduct exploration for certain missing records.

Vigorous and public denial was made—presumably on Executive authority—that any records were missing. Subsequently it developed that several records were missing and most inadequate explanations were supplied. How any public interest could possibly have been prejudiced by affording any opportunity to examine the manner of keeping records of this character has never been satisfactorily explained.

These incidents revealed a disquieting determination to keep entire control of the investigation in the hands of the Committee majority who were thus put in the unusual position of arrogating to themselves the capacity to conduct an impartial and adequate investigation of their own administration. The history of human conduct furnishes few precedents to justify such confidence.

Some of the effects of majority decision as well as gaps in the data and testimony due to other causes illustrate the great difficulty surrounding the work of the Committee.

Secretary Stimson declined to appear on the ground that his health did not permit him to undergo the strain. Access to his diary was denied by majority vote. To accommodate Secretary Stimson because of his illness, Senator Ferguson on March 6, 1946, submitted 176 questions as part of the official record for Secretary Stimson to answer as if propounded in open hearing of the Committee. Secretary Stimson did not answer any of these questions, and the Committee made no effort to insist upon his answering these questions, which were highly pertinent to the inquiry.

Later, Senator Ferguson submitted a supplementary list of 61 questions to be answered in the same manner. Secretary Stimson answered these questions in writing, and his answers are part of the record. These answers did not, however, make up for the deficiencies in the failure to answer the earlier list of 176 questions.

Secretary Hull made three appearances, in the course of which he gave his official version of the matters before the Committee and was briefly examined by the counsel, but minority members of the Committee were not permitted to cross-examine him. When his answers to written interrogatories from Committee members proved unresponsive, there was no way to secure further information from him.

The diary of former Ambassador Joseph C. Grew was likewise denied to the Committee. The assertion of its confidential character was somewhat belied by its submission for examination to certain individuals with a view to its commercial publication.

The denial to the Committee of the Stimson and Grew diaries was particularly obstructive because these principles placed excerpts of the diaries in the record and withheld the rest. This was contrary to the prime rule in American law that if part of a document is put into the record by a witness in his own behalf, the court is entitled to demand the whole of the document. Concerning each of these diaries the Committee, by majority vote, refused to issue subpoenas for their production.

Many messages, probably several hundreds, between Winston Churchill and President Franklin D. Roosevelt received prior to December 7, 1941, were not available to the Committee, although there is good reason to believe that they bore on the gathering crisis. Other messages between Mr Churchill and the British Embassy and American authorities were made available to the Committee, but our Government replies or action taken were not so available.

The former Prime Minister of Great Britain was in this country not on official business while hearings of this Committee were going on. His intimate knowledge of affairs leading up to Pearl Harbor would have cleared up many gaps in the evidence. By majority vote, a request for the appearance of Mr Churchill was refused. President Roosevelt's secretary, Miss Grace Tully, was permitted to determine for herself and the Committee and the country what portions of the official correspondence of the late President had any relevancy to Pearl Harbor. This could hardly be a satisfactory substitute for the responsibility placed upon this Committee.

One of the very important questions concerning the defense of Hawaii dealt with the delays in building airfields and the failure to install radar and other warning devices. Members of the Committee sought to inquire into the performance of one Colonel Theodore Wyman, Jr., in this connection, but the Committee decided against it.

The whole question of whether or not it would have been possible to avoid war by proper diplomatic action and thus avert the Pearl Harbor tragedy was left largely unexplored.

We are permitted only occasional glimpses into this realm but these are fascinating.

A modus vivendi was under discussion with Japan in November 1941 to run for three months. This had been strongly urged by the War and Navy authorities in order to supply absolutely essential time for preparation. Secretaries Stimson and Knox went over the terms of this document and advised Secretary Hull that it adequately protected our interest. Suddenly the modus vivendi was dropped from the agenda and there was substituted the Hull message which was followed shortly after by the attack on Pearl Harbor.

Early on the morning after the delivery of the Hull message Lord Halifax (the British Ambassador) arrived at the State Department. He found Mr Welles in charge and asked him what had become of the modus vivendi. Mr Welles replied that it was dropped because of Chinese lack of interest. Lord Halifax intimated a continuing British interest and Mr Welles significantly replied: "That is not the way London sounded yesterday."

The message from Churchill of the preceding day certainly bears out the Welles' observation. The Committee was told by the State Department that there is no record of any telephone conversations between Mr Churchill and President Roosevelt. This certainly invites inquiry.

The Halifax early morning visit in apparent ignorance of the Churchill message of the day before and of the decision to drop the modus vivendi is not in tune with usual British diplomatic procedure. Whether or not the Japanese would have accepted the modus vivendi must remain a matter of opinion. Whether or not it should have been submitted is a matter on which light might well be shed.

Particularly is this the case when we have the testimony of Gen. George C. Marshall that a delay by the Japanese from December 1941 into January 1942 might have resulted in a change of Japanese opinion as to the wisdom of the attack because of the collapse of the German front before Moscow in December 1941.

Whether or not such a development would have been one to be desired must remain for future investigation when more of the diplomatic history of the closing months of 1941 can be more thoroughly explored.

In short the Committee labored under great difficulties and was not in possession of the full historical record pertinent to the case before it. Nevertheless an investigation was made and an amazing amount of material was developed in the limited time allowed to cover such a vast field. It is the duty of the Committee to render a report, regardless of the inadequacies of evidence, if sufficient facts are at hand to pass on the issues of responsibility for the catastrophe at Pearl Harbor. A careful review of the evidence is convincing enough that these issues can be decided now.

CONCLUSIONS WITH SUPPORTING EVIDENCE

Growing tension with Japan

The course of diplomatic negotiations with Japan during the months preceding December 7, 1941, indicated a growing tension with Japan and after November 26 the immediate imminence of war.

The duty of conducting negotiations with foreign governments from March 4, 1933, to December 7, 1941, was vested in President Franklin D. Roosevelt, under the

Constitution, laws, and established practice of the United States, and he could delegate to the Secretary of State, Cordell Hull, such correspondence and communications relating thereto as he deemed fitting and proper. In respect of matters assigned to him it was the duty of Secretary Hull to keep the President informed of all transactions that were critical in nature and especially those involving the possible use of the armed forces of the United States.

At least as early as October 8, 1940, President Roosevelt believed that affairs had reached such a state that the United States would become involved in a war with Japan. On that day Admiral Richardson asked the President "if we were going to enter the war." According to the admiral's account the President replied:

> that if the Japanese attacked Thailand, or the Kra Peninsula, or the Dutch East Indies we would not enter the war, that if they even attacked the Philippines he doubted whether we would enter the war, but that they (the Japanese) could not always avoid making mistakes and that as the war continued and the area of operations expanded sooner or later they would make a mistake and would enter the war.

In a letter dated January 21, 1941, President Roosevelt informed Ambassador Grew that "our interests are menaced both in Europe and in the Far East. Our strategy of self-defense must be a global strategy" and that "our strategy" must envisage "helping to prevent a closing of channels of communication" between Great Britain and various parts of the world.

Grew's letter dated December 14, 1940, to the President contained this sentence, "the principal point at issue, as I see it, is not whether we call a halt to the Japanese program. But when." The President replied in a letter: "I find myself in decided agreement with your conclusions."

There is additional evidence for the conclusion that in January 1941 President Roosevelt then became convinced that the war was a global war and that his decisions as Chief Executive and Commander in Chief must thenceforward be made with reference to that conviction. This evidence is as follows: Beginning in January 1941 representatives of the American armed forces and representatives of British and Dutch armed forces on the suggestion of the United States started a series of conversations in respect of cooperation against Japan in the Far East. Out of these and subsequent conversations were developed American–British–Dutch war plans for combined operations against Japan if Japanese armed forces started hostile actions against British, Dutch, or American possessions in the Far East. President Roosevelt approved these plans, "except officially," as Admiral Stark testified. The President's commitment to Great Britain was foreshadowed by understandings previously reached between American, British, and Dutch military authorities.

In a memorandum to the President dated November 27, 1941, General Marshall and Admiral Stark stated:

> After consultation with each other United States, British, and Dutch military authorities in the Far East agreed that joint military counteraction against Japan should be undertaken only in case Japan attacks or directly threatens the territory or mandated territory of the United States, the British Commonwealth, or the Netherlands East Indies or should the Japanese move forces into Thailand West of 100 degrees East or South of 10 degrees North, Portuguese Timor, New Caledonia or the Loyalty Islands.

The agreement referred to by Admiral Stark and General Marshall was reached at conferences in Singapore in April 1941 between United States, British, and Dutch military authorities in the Far East. It provided that they would advise their respective Governments to authorize military operations against Japan in the event of any of the following Japanese movements:

(a) A direct act of war by Japanese armed forces against the territory or mandated territory of any of the Associated Powers. It is not possible to define accurately what would constitute "a direct act of war." It is possible for a minor incident to occur which although technically an act of war could be resolved by diplomatic action. It is recognized the decision as to whether such an incident is an act of war must lie with the government concerned.

(b) The movement of the Japanese forces into any part of Thailand to the West of 100 degrees East or to the South of 10 degrees North.

(c) The movement of a large number of Japanese warships or of a convoy of merchant ships escorted by Japanese warships which from its position and course is clearly directed upon the Philippine Islands, the East coast of the Isthmus of Kra of the East coast of Malaya or had crossed the parallel of 6 degrees North between Malaya and the Philippines, a line from the Gulf of Davao to Waigeo Island or the Equator East of Waigeo.

(d) The movement of Japanese forces into Portuguese Timor.

(e) The movement of Japanese forces into New Caledonia or the Loyalty Islands.

The report of the Singapore conversations and the memoranda to the President by Admiral Stark and General Marshall on November 5 and 27, 1941, set forth definite geographic lines, over which a Japanese advance was considered to require armed resistance from the United States, Great Britain, and the Netherlands. One line ran north and south through Thailand. It was parallel to longitude 100 degrees east. A Japanese movement west of it was prohibited. This line protected Burma and the Indian Ocean. Another line ran east and west across the Isthmus of Kra and was parallel with latitude 10 degrees north. A Japanese movement over this line was forbidden. This line in effect protected the Malay Peninsula and Singapore. The Singapore report sets out certain additional lines. One such line was parallel of latitude 6 degrees north and extended between Malaya and the Philippines.

This line protected the Dutch East Indies. They were also protected from Japanese attack, particularly one originating in the Palau Islands, by another line extending from the Gulf of Davao in the Philippines to Waigeo Island in the Dutch East Indies. On December 4, 1941, Admiral Stark, Chief of Naval Operations, sent to the British and Dutch Admiralties his recommendation:

> that if the Dutch authorities considered a warning should
> be given to Japan it should take the form of a declaration
> to Japan that in view of the current situation Japanese
> naval vessels or expeditionary forces crossing the
> Davao–Waigeo line would be considered hostile and
> would be attacked.

While the President did not approve written agreements on these understandings he and the high authorities in Washington acted with the British and Dutch just as if a binding pact had been made. Likewise the Japanese acted upon the same belief that the United States, Britain, and Netherlands East Indies were working together. There is ample evidence in the record to this effect.

Subsequent American diplomatic negotiations with Japan were based upon the principle of cooperation with Great Britain, the Dutch Netherlands, China, and

Australia. No separate over-all plan for the simple defense of American possessions against Japan was developed by the armed forces of the United States between January 1941 and December 7, 1941, with a view to safeguarding American interests separately. After the Japanese attack on December 7, American, British, Dutch, and Australian operations in the Pacific theater were conducted on the cooperative principle which had governed the military and naval conversations and planning between January and December 1941.

The danger of war with Japan formed a principal theme of discussion between President Roosevelt and Prime Minister Churchill at the Atlantic Conference in August 1941, and agreements or understandings reached by President Roosevelt and Prime Minister Churchill at that Conference were based on a common program for dealing with Japan and close cooperation between the United States and Great Britain in diplomatic, military, and naval affairs in respect of the Far East as well as the Atlantic. Their chief understandings as thus far disclosed by official records were three in number:

(1) Common diplomatic actions warning Japan against taking any further steps in dominating neighboring countries by force or threat of force.
(2) Occupation of the Azores by the armed forces of the United States with protective assistance by British armed forces in guarding against a possible Nazi thrust from the mainland.
(3) Cooperation between the United States and Great Britain in "the policing of the world" during a transition period following the close of the war.

Admiral Stark and General Marshall did not approve these Singapore agreements because they were of a "political nature," beyond their authority to sanction. They recommended, however, that these be taken up by the political departments of the governments involved. Further, under other provisions of the Singapore agreements, Britain entrusted the naval defense of her vital interests in the so-called Malay barrier exclusively to the United States and the Dutch. Only three British vessels were allocated to the defense of this area, and these only for escort and patrol. This arrangement was not approved by Stark and Marshall.

After an understanding was reached at the Atlantic Conference on common diplomatic action against Japan—"the President expressed the belief that by adopting this course any further move of aggression on the part of Japan which might result in war could be held off for at least thirty days." The Prime Minister thought that there was a reasonable chance of averting a war in the Pacific.

It is scarcely thinkable that in his discussions with Prime Minister Churchill at the Atlantic Conference in August 1941, President Roosevelt would have assumed that the United States was to cooperate with Great Britain in "the policing of the world" for a transition period after the war, unless he was then certain that at some stage in the development of the war the United States would become involved in it.

In his statement to the Japanese ambassador on Sunday, August 17, 1941, immediately following his return from the Atlantic Conference, President Roosevelt warned Japan against further attempts to dominate "neighboring countries," not merely the possessions of the United States, and used diplomatic language which, according to long-established usages, had only one meaning, namely, that such further attempts would result in a conflict with the United States. His statement read:

> this Government (of the United States) now finds it
> necessary to say to the Government of Japan that if the

Japanese Government takes any further steps in pursuance of a policy or program of military domination by force or threat of force of neighboring countries, the Government of the United States will be compelled to take immediately any and all steps which it may deem necessary toward safeguarding the legitimate rights and interests of the United States and American nationals and toward insuring the safety and security of the United States.

In urging upon the State Department, in September 1941, an acceptance of the Japanese proposal for a conference between President Roosevelt and Premier Konoye, the American ambassador in Tokyo, Joseph Grew, declared that, in his opinion, unless a certain amount of confidence be placed by the United States in the professed sincerity of the Premier Konoye and his supporters in making arrangements for the proposed conference:

> the ambassador does not believe that a new orientation can be successfully created in Japan to lead to a general improving of Japanese–American relations and to the hope that ultimate war may be avoided in the Pacific.

Accordingly, in rejecting the Japanese proposal for this conference, President Roosevelt and Secretary Hull whatever their reasons and however justifiable these reasons may have been, had before them the deliberate judgment of the American ambassador in Tokyo that such action would reduce the chances of peace and increase the probability of war.

The Konoye Cabinet fell on October 16, 1941, after all Japanese efforts to bring about the conference between President Roosevelt and Premier Konoye had failed.

On November 26, 1941, Secretary Hull, with the approval of President Roosevelt, rejected the Japanese pro-

posal of November 20 for a temporary agreement, sometimes called a modus vivendi, and presented to Japan his
memorandum of that date. The Secretary recognized, and
said, that there was then "practically no possibility of an
agreement being achieved with Japan." Having reached
this conclusion, the Secretary, according to his account of
what happened, declared on November 25 and on
November 28, at meetings of high officials of this
Government, "that the matter of safeguarding our national
security was in the hands of the Army and Navy." This was
presumptively a warning to the War Department and the
Navy Department to make ready for war. Accepting it as
such the two Departments sent to General Short and
Admiral Kimmel messages which, the Departments
claimed, ordered the commanders to put into effect a due
alert for war—a possible Japanese attack.

The President, the Secretary of State, the Secretary of
War, and the Secretary of the Navy were, therefore, certainly bound by the duties of their respective offices to be
on the alert day and night after November 26, 1941, for
the receipt of any word or message from Japan and for the
receipt of any intercepts or other information respecting
Japanese designs and intentions that were indicative of a
breach of relations and war. They were also bound by their
duties to alert and to keep on the alert for sudden attack
their immediate subordinates and the outpost commanders
having duties in connection with war operations.

Washington's tactics pending Japanese attack

By November 7, 1941, President Roosevelt and his
Cabinet had reached the unanimous conclusion that war
tension had reached such a point as to convince them that
"the people would back us up in case we struck at Japan
down there (in the Far East)." They then took under consideration "what the tactics would be." Unless Japan

yielded to diplomatic representations on the part of the United States, there were three choices on tactics before the President and the Cabinet: They could wait until Japan attacked; they could strike without a declaration of war by Congress; or the President could lay the issue of peace or war before Congress.

The proposal of an appeal to Congress was not new. So high was the war tension in August 1941, that Prime Minister Churchill, recognizing the constitutional inability of President Roosevelt to declare war, proposed that the President seek authority from Congress to act on certain conditions. The Prime Minister's proposal, contained in his draft of parallel communications to Japan, read:

> If any third power becomes the object of aggression by Japan in consequence of such counter measures or in their support of them the President would have the intention to seek authority from Congress to give aid to such power.

The proposal to incorporate in the American communication to the Japanese Government an announcement of this intention to appeal to Congress was not accepted by President Roosevelt.

Sometime after November 7, 1941, when the President and his Cabinet unanimously agreed that "the country" would back them up in case they struck at Japan in the Far East, high Administration authorities discussed the tactics of an appeal by President Roosevelt to Congress in a special message laying before it the serious danger that was threatening the United States and its interests in the Far East. The officers of the State Department, the Secretary of War, and the Secretary of the Navy took part in drafting the proposed message for the President and their draft, when completed, was accompanied by a memorandum for the President, dated November 29, 1941, initialed by Secretary Hull. In a note sending this draft message to the President, Mr Hull wrote: "I think we agree that you will not send message to Congress until the last stage of our relations, relating to actual hostilities."

The decision against laying the issue before Congress left to the Administration authorities only the tactics of renewing negotiations with Japan (which as to substantive issues had come to an end on November 26) or the tactics of waiting on Japanese decisions and actions.

Mr Roosevelt chose to wait until December 7, 1941, rather than place this grave issue before Congress. This seems clear from the testimony as late as the night before the attack, as follows:

Commander Schulz said that when he delivered the 13-part message to the President on the night of December 6:

> Mr Hopkins then expressed a view that since war was
> undoubtedly going to come at the convenience of the
> Japanese it was too bad that we could not strike the first
> blow and prevent any sort of surprise. The President
> nodded and then said, in effect, "No, we can't do that. We
> are a democracy and a peaceful people." Then he raised his
> voice, and this much I remember definitely. He said: "But
> we have a good record."
>
>   The impression that I got was that we would have to
> stand on that record, we could not make the first overt
> move. We would have to wait until it came.

So imminent was war on November 25 that the President, in a conference with Secretary Hull, Secretary Knox, Secretary Stimson, General Marshall, and Admiral Stark, "brought up the event that we were likely to be attacked perhaps (as soon as) next Monday" (December 1); and the members of the conference discussed the question "How we should maneuver them (the Japanese) into the position of firing the first shot without allowing too much danger to ourselves."

In the diplomatic documents, exhibits, and testimony before the Committee there is a wealth of evidence which underwrites the statement that the tactics of maneuvering the Japanese into "the position of firing the first shot" were followed by high authorities in Washington after November 25, 1941. Examples of such tactics are afforded by:

(a) Secretary Hull's decision, with the approval of President Roosevelt, to discard the proposal for a temporary agreement with Japan without notifying the Secretary of War or the British and Australian representatives in Washington who had collaborated in working out a draft of a memorandum with a view to reaching such an agreement if possible.

(b) The substitution for the proposed modus vivendi of the note of November 26 to Japan, which, as Secretary Hull knew and said at the moment, practically put an end to negotiations with Japan and passed over to the Army and Navy the burden of safeguarding the security of the United States.

Secretary Stimson quoted his diary for November 26 as follows:

> Hull told me over the telephone this morning that he had about made up his mind not to give (make) the proposition that Knox and I passed on the other day to the Japanese but to kick the whole thing over—to tell them that he has no other proposition at all. I called Hull up this morning to tell him [of Chiang Kai-shek's objections to the modus vivendi as set forth in a letter to T.V. Soong and shown by him to Mr Stimson] and asked him

what he wanted me to do about it. He replied as I have said above—that he had made up his mind to give up the whole thing in respect to a truce and to simply tell the Japanese that he had no further action to propose.

(c) The rejection of appeals made to President Roosevelt by General Marshall and Admiral Stark on November 5 and also later on November 7, 1941, for a delay in bringing about a breach with Japan— appeals based on their belief that the Army and Navy were not then ready for a war with Japan.

(d) The orders of the Secretary of War to the effect that General Marshall and Admiral Stark should not put into their memorandum appealing for delay, signed November 27, anything that could be "construed as a recommendation to the President that he request Japan to reopen the conversations."

According to Secretary Hull, the tactics of waiting for the Japanese to fire the first shot was, in a measure, forced upon the Administration by the attachment of a large part of the American people to neutrality as expressed in the neutrality legislation of Congress and by their opposition to involvement in war in the Far East as well as elsewhere.

This view Secretary Hull expressed in his statement to the Committee and it is set forth more fully by other documents before the Committee, particularly the State Department's publication: *Peace and War: United States Foreign Policy 1931–41*, especially Chapter 1.

In this chapter the State Department explains that the President and Secretary Hull were hampered in the pursuit of the foreign policy they had "clearly" decided upon—at a date not fixed by the Secretary—on account of the opposition by "much of public opinion" in the United States. In this chapter the State Department also explains that:

Our foreign policy during the decade under consideration (1931–41) necessarily had to move within the framework of a gradual evolution of public opinion in the United States away from the idea of isolation expressed in "neutrality" legislation. The pages (in the volume) which follow show the slow march of the United States from an attitude of illusory aloofness toward worldwide forces endangering America to a position in the forefront of the United Nations that are now (1943) making common cause against an attempt at world conquest unparalleled alike in boldness of conception and in brutality of operation.

It is a serious question whether the President and his advisers were justified in making the conclusions that the country would support them for war; and whether actions taken by them upon their own opinion without placing the matter before Congress was in violation of their responsibilities under the Constitution and laws of the land.

Having considered, without agreeing upon the proposition, that a message on the war situation should be sent to Congress, the President and the Secretary of State, the Secretary of War, and the Secretary of the Navy pursued, from November 25 to December 7, the tactics of waiting for the firing of "the first shot" by the Japanese.

Nothing that indicates any easing of the tension between the United States and Japan appears in the records of the exchanges with the Japanese representatives in Washington between November 27 and December 6, inclusive. On the contrary, relations were rapidly deteriorating. It was the general opinion among Washington authorities that the question was no longer "would Japan attack," but "when and where."

On November 28, President Roosevelt said to Secretary Stimson that he could see only three alternatives before him in the situation: "first, to do nothing; second, to make something in the nature of an ultimatum again, stating a point beyond which we would fight; third, to fight at once."

As late as December 2, President Roosevelt seemed to be still considering the subject of a message to Congress. Secretary Stimson recorded on that day: The President "is quite settled, I think, that he will make a message to the Congress and will, perhaps, back that up with a speech to the country." On December 2, he was also considering the possibility of a message to the Japanese Emperor.

With these possibilities of tactics before him, the President fully abandoned the three projects: another ultimatum, fighting at once, sending a message to Congress. He only turned to the fourth possibility—sending an appeal to the Japanese Emperor—after it was too late; that is, after 9 p.m. on the night of December 6, when the White House had been alerted that the Japanese answer to our note of November 26 was coming in and being decoded and his naval aide was on special duty to receive and deliver it to him. Hence, in such respects, he adhered to his first alternative, that of waiting for Japanese action.

Failure of Washington to warn Hawaiian commanders

The appropriate high authorities in Washington had the organization for working in such close cooperation during the days immediately prior to the Japanese attack on December 7 that they had every opportunity to make sure that identical and precise instructions warranted by the imminence of war went to the Hawaiian commanders.

For the purpose of taking concerted actions in fulfillment of the duties imposed upon them, authorities in Washington formed two groups or organizations with a view to coordinating the operations of the civil and military branches of the executive department. If these groups were so loosely constituted as not to deserve the name of organizations, this was due to a failure on the part of the members to make them effective bodies for the discharge of their coordinating responsibilities.

The first of these two groups consisted of the Secretary of State, Secretary of War, Secretary of the Navy, the Chief of Staff, and the Chief of Naval Operations. Sometimes it was called colloquially the "War Council."

The second group included the President, Secretary of State, Secretary of War, Secretary of the Navy, usually the Chief of Staff and the Chief of Naval Operations, and occasionally the commanding general of the Air Force, General Arnold. This group was sometimes colloquially called the "War Cabinet."

The use of these terms—"War Council" and "War Cabinet"—while the country was still at peace seems to indicate that high civil and military authorities in Washington were thinking in terms of war and should have been more alert to the probable events of war, such as an attack upon our most important outpost and fleet in the Pacific. Each of these groups or organizations:

> was a sort of clearinghouse for information, a gathering place for discussion of policies, so that each of the independent actors in the scene would know what was going on and would have information to guide him in making his own decisions that were more or less independent, but at the same time somewhat dependent on the action of other members of the group.

If it be argued that these groups were loosely constituted and met irregularly and informally and hence were not organizations in the strict sense of the term [they met once a week at least and had other irregular and additional meetings], it remains a fact that they existed for the purposes described. Furthermore, if, owing to their loose constitution, they did not discharge their duties efficiently, it also remains a fact that the President had the power, and the corresponding duty, to transform either or both of these groups into positive organizations with positive obligations in respect of exchanging information, making decisions, coordinating the civil and military branches of the executive department, and framing orders to outpost commanders.

At all events, these groups had every opportunity to make sure that identical and precise instructions warranted by the imminence of war went out to the Hawaiian commanders and the President had the power and duty to see that this was done directly or through the agency of these groups, especially the second—the "War Cabinet."

Intercepted information

Through the Army and Navy intelligence services extensive information was secured respecting Japanese war plans and designs, by intercepted and decoded Japanese secret messages, which indicated the growing danger of war and increasingly after November 26 the imminence of a Japanese attack.

With extraordinary skill, zeal, and watchfulness the intelligence services of the Army Signal Corps and the Navy Office of Naval Communications broke Japanese codes and intercepted messages between the Japanese Government and its spies and agents and ambassadors in all parts of the world and supplied the high authorities in Washington reliable secret information respecting Japanese designs, decisions, and operations at home, in the United States, and in other countries. Although there were delays in the translations of many intercepts, the intelligence services had furnished to those high authorities a large number of Japanese messages which clearly indicated the growing resolve of the Japanese Government on war before December 7, 1941.

Incidentally, it was a matter of great imprudence for the State and War Departments to permit so large a number (200) of Japanese consular representatives at so important a naval base as Hawaii. Much of the espionage involved in the intercepts emanated from this consular group in Hawaii.

Four volumes laid before the Committee contain hundreds of these messages—including in some cases comment and interpretations. No person has any intellectual or moral right to pass judgment on the question of responsibility for Pearl Harbor who has not read, compared, studied, and interpreted all of these documents.

The President, and the other officials receiving the intercepted messages in Washington prior to December 7, 1941, considered it likely that Japan would attack the United States. At a meeting of the President and his so-called War Council on November 25, 1941, according to Mr Stimson's notes, the President stated: "That we were likely to be attacked perhaps (as soon as) next Monday."

There was abundant evidence in the intercepted messages that Japan intended to attack the United States. Japan had fixed a dead-line date of November 25, extended to November 29 for reaching diplomatic agreement with the United States. There were at least six Japanese messages emphasizing this dead-line. If the dead-line date passed without agreement, the Japanese Government advised her ambassadors in Washington: "Things are automatically going to happen."

The necessity for agreement by the dead-line date was stressed by Japan in these terms: "The fate of our Empire hangs by the slender thread of a few days"; "We gambled the fate of our land on the throw of this die." On

November 26, 1941, prior to the advanced "dead-line" date, the United States Government delivered to Japan a diplomatic note, which the intercepted messages revealed Japan considered to be a "humiliating proposal," impossible of acceptance. The intercepted diplomatic messages further revealed that Japan expected to "rupture" negotiations with the United States when she replied to the American note of November 26.

To prevent the United States from becoming unduly suspicious, Japan instructed her envoys in Washington to keep up a pretext of continuing negotiations until this Japanese reply was ready for delivery. A message from the Japanese Government to its ambassador in Berlin, sent on November 30, was intercepted and translated by the Navy in Washington on December 1. In this message the Japanese ambassador was instructed to:

> immediately interview Chancellor Hitler and Foreign
> Minister Ribbentrop and confidentially communicate to
> them a summary of developments. Say very secretly to
> them that there is extreme danger that war may suddenly
> break out between the Anglo-Saxon nations and Japan
> through some clash of arms and add the time of the
> breaking out of this war may come quicker than anyone
> dreams.

The President regarded this message as of such interest that he retained a copy of it, contrary to the usual practice in handling the intercepted messages. On December 2, 1941, elaborate instructions from Japan were intercepted dealing in precise detail with the method of internment of American and British nationals in Asia "on the outbreak of war with England and the United States."

The probability that the Pacific Fleet would be attacked at Pearl Harbor was clear from the "bomb plot" available in Washington as early as October 9, 1941, and related Japanese messages. It will aid in obtaining a clear understanding of these important messages if the principal intercepted communications are set forth in full. They are:

From: Tokyo (Toyoda)
To: Honolulu
September 24, 1941
#83
Strictly secret

Henceforth, we would like to have you make reports concerning vessels along the following lines insofar as possible:

1. The waters (of Pearl Harbor) are to be divided roughly into five sub-areas. (We have no objections to your abbreviating as much as you like.)

Area A. Waters between Ford Island and the Arsenal.

Area B. Waters adjacent to the Island south and west of Ford Island. (This area is on the opposite side of the Island from Area A.)

Area C. East Loch.

Area D. Middle Loch.

Area E. West Loch. And the communicating water routes.

2. With regard to warships and aircraft carriers, we would like to have you report on those at anchor (these are not so important), tied up at wharves, buoys, and in the docks. (Designate types and classes briefly. If possible we would like to have you make mention of the fact when there are two or more vessels alongside the same wharf.)

From: Honolulu (Kita)
To: Washington
September 29, 1941
Circular #041
Honolulu to Tokyo #178
Re your #083
(Strictly secret)

The following codes will be used hereafter to designate the location vessels:

1. Repair dock in Navy Yard (The repair basin referred to in my message Washington #48): KS.
2. Navy Dock in the Navy Yard (The Ten Ten Pier): KT.
3. Moorings in the vicinity of Ford Island: FV.
4. Alongside in Ford Island: FG. (East and west sides will be differentiated by A and B respectively.)
Relayed to Washington, San Francisco.

From: Tokyo (Togo)
To: Honolulu (Riyoji)
November 15, 1941
#111

As relations between Japan and the United States are most critical, make your ships in harbor report irregular, but at a rate of twice a week. Although you already are no doubt aware, please take extra care to maintain secrecy.

From: Tokyo (Togo)
To: Honolulu
November 18, 1941
#113

Please report on the following areas as to vessels anchored therein:
Area "N", Pearl Harbor, Manila Bay[1], and the Areas Adjacent thereto.
(Make your investigation with great secrecy.)

From: Tokyo (Togo)
To: Honolulu
November 20, 1941
#111 Strictly secret

Please investigate comprehensively the fleet-bases in the neighborhood of the Hawaiian military reservation.

From: Tokyo
To: Honolulu
November 29, 1941
#122

We have been receiving reports from you on ship movements, but in future will you also report even where there are no movements.

From: Honolulu (Kita)
To: Tokyo
November 18, 1941
#222

1. The warship at anchor in the harbor on the 15th were as I told you in my #219[2] on that day.
Area A[3] A battleship of the Oklahoma class entered and one tanker left port.

---

[1] Probably means Mamala Bay.
[2] Available, dated November 14. Code under study.
[3] Waters between Ford Island and the Arsenal.

Area C[4] Three warships of the heavy cruiser class were at anchor.

2. On the 17th the *Saratoga* was not in the harbor. The carrier *Enterprise*, or some other vessel, was in area C. Two heavy cruisers of the Chicago class, one of the Pensacola class were tied up at docks KS. Four merchant vessels were at anchor in Area D[5].

3. At 10 a.m. on the morning of the 17th, eight destroyers were observed entering the harbor. Their course was as follows: In a single file at a distance of 1,000 meters apart at a speed of 3 knots per hour, they moved into Pearl Harbor. From the entrance of the harbor through area B to the buoys in area C, to which they were moored, they changed course five times, each time roughly 30 degrees. The elapsed time was 1 hour; however; one of these destroyers entered area A after passing the water reservoir on the eastern side.

Relayed to—.

In the "bomb plot" message of September 24, 1941, the Japanese Government gave detailed instructions to its consul general in Hawaii as to the character of report it required concerning vessels in Pearl Harbor. This dispatch was decoded and translated in Washington on October 9, 1941.

On September 29, 1941, the Japanese consul in Hawaii replied to his government. He established a system of symbols to be used in designating the location of vessels at key points in Pearl Harbor. This dispatch was decoded and translated in Washington on October 10, 1941.

On November 15, 18, 20, and 29 the Japanese Government urgently called for information about the

---

[4] East Loch.
[5] Middle Loch.

location of ships in Pearl Harbor. These dispatches were intercepted, decoded, and translated in Washington on December 3, 4, 5, and 6, 1941.

The "bomb plot" message, and those messages relating to Pearl Harbor which followed it, meant that the ships of the Pacific Fleet in Pearl Harbor were marked for a Japanese attack. No other American harbor was divided into sub-areas by Japan. And no other American harbor had such a large share of the fleet to protect.

In no other area did Japan seek information as to whether two or more vessels were alongside the same wharf. Prior to the "bomb plot" message Japanese espionage in Hawaii was directed to ascertain the general whereabouts of the American fleet, whether at sea or in port. With the "bomb plot" message Japan inaugurated a new policy directed to Pearl Harbor and to no other place, in which information was no longer sought merely as to the general whereabouts of the fleet, but as to the presence of particular ships in particular areas of the harbor. In the period immediately preceding the attack Japan required such reports even when there was no movement of ships in and out of Pearl Harbor. The reports which Japan thus sought and received had a useful purpose only in planning and executing an attack upon the ships in port. These reports were not just the work of enthusiastic local spies gathering meticulous details in an excess of zeal. They were the product of instructions emanating from the Government of Japan in Tokyo. Officers of the high command in Washington have admitted before us that the "bomb plot" message, if correctly evaluated, meant an attack on ships of the Pacific Fleet in Pearl Harbor.

On October 9, 1941, Lieutenant Commander Kramer of Naval Intelligence in Washington promptly distributed the Pearl Harbor "bomb plot" message to the President, the Secretary of the Navy, the Chief of Naval Operations,

Admiral Stark, the Director of Naval Communications, the Director of War Plans, and the Director of Naval Intelligence. It bore the location "interesting message" on a gist or flag. It was accompanied by a summary of its contents as follows:

> Tokyo directs special reports on ships in Pearl Harbor which is divided into five areas for the purpose of showing exact locations.

Military Intelligence through Colonel Bratton delivered the "bomb plot" message to the Secretary of War, the Chief of Staff, and the chief of the War Plans Division. The message was discussed several times by Colonel Bratton, Chief of the Far Eastern Section, Military Intelligence Division, War Department General Staff, and with his opposite numbers in the Navy Department. They discussed the possible significance of the message, as implicating a plan for an air attack on ships in Pearl Harbor. In the course of these discussions officers in Naval Intelligence stated that the Japanese were wasting their time in getting such meticulous detail about the location of ships in Pearl Harbor because the fleet would not be in Pearl Harbor when the emergency arose.

Simple reason in evaluating these "bomb plot" messages should have discovered their significance.

1. Such meticulous detail was not needed to enable Japan to keep track of the American fleet for general purposes.
2. The messages were sent to Tokyo obviously for use originating from there—air or sea attack.
3. The messages couldn't be for sabotage. Sabotage is an on-the-spot affair. Saboteurs have to be in Hawaii. They get their information direct by local observation. Therefore, they needed no bomb plot.

4.   The only purpose could be for air attack, submarine attack, direct invasion—all external operations.
5.   Had Washington so evaluated this bomb plot, it could have seen this significance and warned the commanders at Hawaii. Washington authorities failed to do so or if they did in fact evaluate it, they failed to pass the information on to the Hawaiian commanders.

The commander of a fleet (in this case Admiral Kimmel) has custody of the fleet; he is at all times materially interested in its safety. The commander of a naval base (in this case General Short) has the duty of protecting the fleet when it is at his base. Any information showing specific hostile interest in that fleet or in the harbor where the fleet is anchored is basic information for the commander of the fleet and the commander of the naval base.

In Washington, long prior to December 7, 1941, Army and Navy Intelligence officers, the Chief of Naval Operations, the Army Chief of Staff, and other high authorities gained vital information (the "bomb plot" messages) from intercepted Japanese communications affecting the fleet and the defense of the naval base at Hawaii. They gained it from sources of information not available to Admiral Kimmel and General Short.

In these circumstances, it was the express duty of the Washington authorities to pass this information in its original form on to Admiral Kimmel and General Short. The information was of such a specific character and so directly related to the fleet and naval base that Washington authorities were not justified in keeping to themselves or in evaluating it in any manner which would dilute or generalize the significance of the messages in their original form. Washington authorities failed in this, a prime responsibility in their relations with the outpost commanders.

In the days immediately preceding Pearl Harbor, Japan made no effort to conceal the movements or presence of her naval forces in Southeast Asia. The movements of her troops in Indo-China at that time were the subject of diplomatic exchanges between the United States and Japan. Yet the intercepts showed that some Japanese plan went into effect automatically on November 29, from which Japan hoped to divert American suspicion by a pretext of continued negotiations. The Pearl Harbor "bomb plot" messages gave some hint of what might follow "automatically."

Only the President and his top advisers in Washington had this information. Other messages intercepted later were even more revealing. These were the intercepted Japanese messages distributed in Washington on Saturday afternoon and evening, December 6, and several hours before the blow fell on Sunday morning, December 7. These were:

1. The "pilot message." This was a message from Japan to her ambassadors in Washington advising them that the Japanese reply to the American note of November 26 was ready and being sent to them in 14 parts; that it was to be treated with great secrecy pending instructions as to the time of its delivery; and that the time for its delivery was to be fixed in a separate message.
2. The first 13 parts of the Japanese reply. This included all but the last paragraph of the Japanese note handed to the Secretary of State on December 7.
3. The fourteenth and last paragraph of the Japanese reply, and the message to the Japanese ambassadors which fixed the time for delivery of the Japanese note as 1 p.m. Washington time, December 7.

Prior to December 7, 1941, a great volume of secret information obtained by American and other intelligence services from intercepted Japanese messages was available in Washington with which to gage the designs, intentions, and operations of Japan relative to the United States. This information was distributed to high authorities in Washington and practically none of it was passed on to the commanders in Hawaii although it bore directly on their responsibilities in the defense of their outpost.

Army and Navy information which indicated the growing imminence of war was delivered to the highest authorities in charge of national preparedness for meeting an attack, among others, the President, the Secretaries of State, War, and Navy, and the Chief of Staff and the Chief of Naval Operations.

The "Magic" intelligence was regarded as preeminently confidential and the policy with respect to its restricted distribution was dictated by a desire to safeguard the secret that the Japanese diplomatic codes were being broken. Delivery of the English texts of the intercepted messages was limited, within the War Department, to the Secretary of War, the Chief of Staff, the Chief of the War Plans Division, and the Chief of the Military Intelligence Division; within the Navy, to the Secretary of the Navy, the Chief of Naval Operations, the Chief of the War Plans Division, and the Director of Naval Intelligence; to the State Department; and to the President's naval aide for transmittal to the President. By agreement between the Army and Navy in Washington, the Army was responsible for distribution of "Magic" within the War Department and to the State Department; the Navy for distribution within the Navy Department and to the White House.

The President requested the original raw messages in English, examining them personally, and on December 6 had his naval aide on special night duty to receive and deliver them to him.

The dissemination of "Magic" materials did not include the commanders at Hawaii, but on a few occasions material derived therefrom was dispatched by the Navy Department to Admiral Kimmel. The War Department did not send the "Magic" to the field. A large amount of other intelligence obtained from various sources within and without the country was not sent to either of the commanders in Hawaii.

Expectation and probability of a Japanese attack

Judging by the military and naval history of Japan, high authorities in Washington and the commanders in Hawaii had good grounds for expecting that in starting war the Japanese Government would make a surprise attack on the United States.

There is no evidence in the record before the Committee that President Roosevelt, Secretary Hull, Secretary Stimson, and/or Secretary Knox expected at any time prior to December 7 a formal declaration of war on the United States by Japan in case the diplomatic negotiations came to a break. Indeed, all the evidence bearing on expectations in Washington as to Japan's probable methods of making war point to the belief of the Administration that Japan would begin with a surprise attack.

For example, Secretary Hull on November 25 and November 28 at a meeting of "high officials," when he stated that the matter of safeguarding our national security was in the hands of the Army and Navy, "expressed his judgment that any plans for our military defense would include the assumption that the Japanese might make the element of surprise a central point in their strategy, and also might attack at various points simultaneously with a view to demoralizing efforts of defense and of coordination for purposes thereof."

Speaking to Ambassador Halifax on November 29, Secretary Hull said that it would be a "serious mistake to make plans of resistance without including the possibility that Japan may move suddenly and with every possible element of surprise that the Japanese recognize that their course of unlimited conquest is a desperate gamble and requires the utmost boldness and risk."

Ambassador Grew reported to Hull on November 3: "Japan may resort with dangerous and dramatic suddenness to measures which might make inevitable war with the United States."

∘◦◊◊◊◦∘

Neither the diplomatic negotiations nor the intercepts and other information respecting Japanese designs and operations in the hands of the United States authorities warranted those authorities in excluding from defense measures or from orders to the Hawaiian commanders the probability of an attack on Hawaii. On the contrary, there is evidence to the effect that such an attack was, in terms of strategy, necessary from the Japanese point of view and in fact highly probable, and that President Roosevelt was taking the probability into account—before December 7.

The fleet was stationed at Pearl Harbor in a large measure, if not entirely, for the purpose of exercising a deterring effect on the aggressive propensities of the Japanese Government during the diplomatic negotiations, and of making the Government more likely to yield to the diplomatic representations of the United States in matters of policy.

This was done contrary to the advice of the Commander in Chief of the US Fleet, Admiral Richardson (who was removed because of protest on that issue), and with which Admiral William D. Leahy, former

Chief of Naval Operations agreed. The fleet could produce this effect only as an instrument of war that constituted a potential threat to the Japanese; that is, a powerful instrument which could be used effectively to strike Japanese armed forces if they moved too far southward in the direction of British, Dutch, and/or American possessions in that region.

Having determined to move far southward and having moved far on the way early in December toward that region, the Japanese were warned by every principle of sound naval strategy to destroy, if possible, the American fleet at Hawaii on their left flank.

As Prime Minister Churchill said, in an address to the House of Commons on January 27, 1942, with reference to the Atlantic Conference and British strategic decisions as time went on after that Conference:

> It must also be remembered that over the whole Pacific scene brooded the great power of the United States Fleet, concentrated at Hawaii. It seemed very unlikely that Japan would attempt the distant invasion of the Malay Peninsula, the assault upon Singapore, and the attack upon the Dutch East Indies, while leaving behind them in their rear this great American Fleet.

President Roosevelt recognized this strategic consideration as shown by his message to Chiang Kai-shek as follows:

> Meanwhile we are exchanging views with the British Government in regard to the entire situation and the tremendous problems which are presented, with a view to effective coordinating of efforts in the most practicable way possible.
>
> Indirectly influencing that situation: American military and naval defensive forces in the Philippine Islands, which

are being steadily increased, and the United States Fleet at Hawaii, lying as they do along the flank of any Japanese military movement into China from Indo-China, are ever present and significant factors in the whole situation, as are the increasing British and Dutch defensive preparations in their territories to the south by President Roosevelt and transmitted through Ambassador Hu Shih to Chiang Kai-shek.

High authorities in Washington definitely knew from a message received from Ambassador Winant in London at 10:40 a.m. December 6, 1941 (Washington time) that two large Japanese forces had been seen sailing toward the Kra Peninsula and were distant only 14 hours in time. Washington authorities should have known, therefore, that this would bring the strategic principle of what to do about Hawaii into immediate military calculations. They took no steps to alert Hawaii.

The Japanese were fully aware of this strategic principle in December 1941, as their attack on Pearl Harbor demonstrated.

During the weeks preceding December 7, what was the attitude of high authorities in Washington with regard to the probability of Japanese action against Pearl Harbor in accordance with this strategic principle?

Some of those high authorities thought that the Japanese would not take the risk of such an attack. Indeed those authorities were seriously lacking in information respecting the progress and state of Japanese military and naval preparedness and equipment, and they were unaware of the degree to which the Japanese were equipped to attack the American fleet and military installations at Pearl Harbor. The State Department seemed to labor under the impression that the United States could defeat Japan in a few weeks. Judging by the testimony and documents before the Committee, most of the high authorities in Washington, especially after the Atlantic Conference in August 1941, so concentrated their attention on American–British–Australian–Dutch plans for combined actions against the Japanese in southeastern Asia that they failed to give sufficient, if any, careful consideration to the strategic principle which enjoined the Japanese to destroy, if they could, the American fleet at Hawaii on their left flank before advancing too deeply into southeastern waters.

Nevertheless the possibility, indeed the probability, of a Japanese attack on Pearl Harbor had entered into the calculations of high authorities in Washington and the commanders at Pearl Harbor for years, months, and days before December 7, 1941.

The whole raison d'etre of the powerful naval and military installations in Hawaii, as publicly announced, was defense against a Japanese attack. Preparations for defense against attack necessarily implied the possibility of an attack. American war plans and maneuvers in the Hawaiian area for years prior to December 7, 1941, took into full account the probability of a Japanese attack by air.

None of the Army and Navy witnesses before the Committee admitted they had neglected the possibility— or the probability—of a Japanese attack on Pearl Harbor during the period prior to December. On the contrary, they testified that they had consistently reckoned with the possibility, even when they minimized the probability.

Intercepts of Japanese messages made by the Army and Navy intelligence services showed high authorities in Washington that the Japanese Government had ordered its agents in Hawaii to report on American military and naval installations and ship movements in that region. They also required reports on "lack of movements."

It is true that owing to neglect or delays in Washington some of these messages were not translated prior to December 7, 1941, but enough messages had been translated to provide copious information to high authorities in Washington. Delays in translations were not due to lack of congressional appropriations.

Witnesses before the Committee, it may be noted, in extenuation of their lack of emphasis on the probability of an attack on Pearl Harbor, called attention to the fact that Japanese agents were also reporting on the military and naval installations of the United States at Panama, the Philippines, the west coast, and other points. But to men, competent, careful, and watchful, men alert on their all-around and indivisible responsibility, this fact provided no excuse whatever for minimizing the probability of an attack on Pearl Harbor any more than at any other American outpost. Nor does it excuse the failure of Washington authorities to note that far greater detail was being asked for by the Japanese about Hawaii at a time when Japanese movements in the Southeastern Pacific had to contend with the strategic position of Hawaii where the real American striking force, the fleet, rested.

A full review of the testimony and documents before the Committee confirms the conclusion reached by the Army Pearl Harbor Board, after its survey of relevant facts: "We must therefore conclude that the responsible authorities, the Secretary of the Navy and the Chief of Staff in Washington, down to the generals and admirals in Hawaii, all expected an air attack before Pearl Harbor."

As a general statement, when testifying after the Pearl Harbor attack, they did not expect it. Apparently the only person who was not surprised was the Secretary of War, Mr Stimson who testified: "Well, I was not surprised!"

Obligation and responsibility of Washington high authorities

The knowledge of Japanese designs and intentions in the hands of the President and the Secretary of State led them to the conclusion at least 10 days before December 7 that an attack by Japan within a few days was so highly probable as to constitute a certainty and, having reached this conclusion, the President, as Commander in Chief of the Army and Navy, was under obligation to instruct the Secretary of War and Secretary of the Navy to make sure that the outpost commanders put their armed forces on an all-out alert for war.

Besides the knowledge of Japanese designs and operations which the President and the Secretary of State acquired from their diplomatic negotiations with Japan, they also had the knowledge of Japanese designs and operations made available to them by the Army and Navy intelligence services. This additional knowledge could only serve to fortify the conviction already reached as early as November 25, namely, that a Japanese attack was near at hand or to use President Roosevelt's own words: "we were likely to be attacked perhaps as soon as Monday" (December 1).

The nature of the additional information placed at the disposal of the President and Secretary of State by the Army and Navy Intelligence Service is indicated by the citations of Army and Navy intercepts of Japanese messages.

As early as September 24, 1941, Washington authorities knew that Japanese agents in Hawaii were instructed to divide the waters of Pearl Harbor into five sub-areas and later to report to Tokyo regularly on ships in the Harbor, ship movements, and also to report even though there were no ship movements. These and other Japanese messages requested information also on military installations, and American preparedness materiel, defensive practices, including air reconnaissance, and other matters of vital importance to Japanese armed forces in case they made an attack on Pearl Harbor.

From a message from Tokyo to Washington, dated and translated on November 28, authorities in Washington learned that the Japanese Government regarded the American note of November 26 as "a humiliating proposal," and that "Japan cannot use it as a basis for negotiations." They further learned from this same Tokyo message that the Japanese answer would be sent to the Japanese ambassadors in Washington in two or three days, "after which negotiations will be de facto ruptured."

From a message from Tokyo to Berlin, dated November 30 and translated December 1, high authorities in Washington learned that the American note of November 26 was considered by the Japanese Government as "insulting" and that the Japanese Government regarded negotiations with the United States as "ruptured-broken," and that "the time of the breaking out of this war may come quicker than anyone dreams."

∞◦⬦◦∞

Although the knowledge gained from these and other items of information was sufficient to warn high authorities in Washington that Japan was on the verge of starting hostilities, reference should be made in this connection to the so-called "winds" messages concerning which there had been much dispute and no little mystery. The story, though long, may be abbreviated here.

Colonel Otis Sadtler testified before the Army Pearl Harbor Board that about November 20, 1941, a Japanese message was intercepted notifying nationals that another message was to come indicating whether war, if launched, would be against the United States, Great Britain, or Russia or any combination of them. The first message stated that the second or "activating" message to come would indicate by reference to the directions of the winds and weather the names of the countries against which war would be started. The Army Pearl Harbor Board also had evidence to the effect that the second or "activating" message from Japan had come and that it meant "War with England, War with America, Peace with Russia." According to the Board's report:

> This original message has now disappeared from the Navy files and cannot be found. It was in existence just after Pearl Harbor and was collected with other messages for submission to the Roberts Commission.
>
> Copies were in existence in various places but they have all disappeared.

The evidence before this Committee bearing on the interception of the activating message from Tokyo and on the contention that it indicated hostilities between Japan and the Anglo-American combination covers hundreds of pages. Admittedly the evidence is confusing and conflicting, but after reviewing it, Admiral Royal E. Ingersoll, deputy to Admiral Harold Stark, testified before the Hart Inquiry to questions 68 and 69:

> *68.* Q. During November or December '41 were you cognizant of a special code which the Japanese had arranged under which they were to inform their nationals concerning against what nations they would make aggressive movements by means of a partial weather report?
>
> *A.* Yes; I do recall such messages.

69. Q. Do you recall having seen on or about 4 December the broadcast directive thus given indicating that the Japanese were about to attack both Britain and the United States?

A. Yes.

Admiral Ingersoll, Deputy to Admiral Harold Stark at Washington, and Admiral Turner, Navy operations officer at Washington, both stated they did not know until 1945 about the allegation that there had been no "wind" execute message. Even if the "wind" execute message they saw was a false one they believed it true at the time and should have acted accordingly.

If, however, the receipt of the activating "winds" message be wholly discounted, such discounting in no way affects the other items of unmistakable evidence which demonstrates that high authorities in Washington had sufficient knowledge of Japanese designs to convince them before the attack that war with Japan was an imminent certainty.

From a message from Tokyo to Washington, dated December 2 and translated December 3, high authorities in Washington learned that the Japanese Government had ordered its Washington Embassy to destroy all codes, except one, and all secret documents. (One code machine was to be kept for use in the final negotiations which ended in the rupture of relations on December 7.)

From a message dated December 6 and translated on December 6, sometime in the afternoon, Washington authorities learned that the Japanese Government had notified the Japanese Embassy in Washington that a memorandum for the United States would be sent in 14 parts and to be prepared to present it—the memorandum that would make a rupture in relations with the United States.

Messages serving as guides to procedure in the matter of this 14-part message follow:

(Secret)

From: Tokyo
To: Washington
December 7, 1941
(Urgent—Very Important)
#907 To be handled in Government Code
Re my #902

Will the Ambassador please submit to the United States Government (if possible to the Secretary of State) our reply to the United States at 1:00 p.m., on the 7th, your time.

Trans. 12/7/41 (S)

Army 25850

(Secret)

From: Tokyo
To: Washington
December 6, 1941
#904
Re my #902

There is really no need to tell you this, but in the preparation of the aide memoire be absolutely sure not to use a typist or any other person. Be most extremely cautious in preserving secrecy.

Trans. 12-6-41 (S)

Army 25844
JD: 7144

(Secret)

From: Tokyo
To: Washington
December 7, 1941
(Extremely Urgent)
#910

After deciphering part 14 of my #902 a and also #907 b, #908 c and #909 d, please destroy at once the remaining cipher machine and all machine codes. Dispose in like manner also secret documents.

Trans. 12/7/41 (S)

The "pilot message" was filed in Tokyo at 6:56 a.m. Washington time December 6; it was intercepted by the Navy by 7:20 a.m. Washington time December 6, and forwarded to the Navy Department. It was sent by the Navy to the Army for decryption and translation about noon, Washington time, on December 6. It was decrypted, translated, and distributed about 3 p.m., Washington time, by the Army, to Mr Hull, Mr Stimson, General Marshall, the Chief of the War Plans Division, General Gerow, and the Chief of Military Intelligence, General Miles. In the Navy Department the Director of Naval Intelligence—Admiral Wilkinson—received the so-called "pilot message" prior to 6 p.m., Washington time, on December 6. He had previously told his subordinates to be on the lookout for the Japanese reply and felt sure that he gave instructions that the "pilot message" was to be delivered to Admiral Stark. Admiral Turner, Chief of the War Plans Division in the Office of the Chief of Naval Operations, received the "pilot message" in the evening of December 6. Admiral Stark and General Marshall each denies that on December 6 he had knowledge of the "pilot message." We find on the testimony of General Miles and Colonel Bratton that the "pilot message" was delivered to General Marshall during the afternoon of December 6, 1941.

In late afternoon or early evening of December 6, American Naval Communications intercepted, decoded, and translated the first 13 parts of this memorandum from the Japanese Government to the State Department—the answer to the United States' note to Japan on November 26. The translation of these 13 parts was presented to President Roosevelt between 9 and 10 o'clock that evening. After he had read the 13 parts, the President said in substance: "This means war."

The evidence indicated that the first 13 parts were read on the evening of December 6 by, particularly, the President, Mr Harry Hopkins, Secretary Knox, Admiral Ingersoll, Admiral Turner, Admiral Wilkinson, Admiral Beardall, General Miles, Captain Kramer, and Colonel Bratton.

Owing to the practice of making decisions by war cabinets, councils, joint committees, and individuals, the official responsibility of each man was so blurred that each man became indifferent to his own individual responsibility. A good example of this is Admiral Turner's assumption that so long as Admiral Wilkinson, Admiral Ingersoll, and Secretary Knox had seen the 13-part message, "I did not believe it was my function to take any action." No one took action that night; all waited for the next day.

When Mr Knox received the message he called Mr Stimson and Mr Hull and arranged a conference with them for Sunday morning at 10 a.m. Mr Stimson asked the Navy Department on Saturday evening to furnish him by 9 a.m. Sunday morning the following information:

Compilation of men-of-war in Far East: British, American, Japanese, Dutch, Russian; also compilation of American men-of-war in Pacific Fleet, with locations, with a list of American men-of-war in the Atlantic without locations.

Admirals Stark, Ingersoll, and the Secretary of the Navy were consulted about this request. The compilation showed that practically all the ships of the Pacific Fleet were in Pearl Harbor.

The Secretary of the Navy stated that: On many occasions the obligation of an officer was weakened by intermeddling of superiors. President Roosevelt, himself, often directed detailed operations for which field commanders were responsible. An example of this occurred in connection with an order on December 2, 1941, which the Chief of Naval Operations sent to the Commander in Chief of the Asiatic Fleet, commencing as follows: "President directs that the following be done as soon as possible and within two days if possible after receipt this dispatch."

The President's directions were that the Commander in Chief of the Asiatic Fleet was to charter three small vessels to form a "defensive information patrol." The minimum requirements to establish these ships as United States men-of-war would suffice in manning them. These requirements were command by a naval officer and the mounting of a small gun and one machine gun. The employment of Filipino crews with the minimum number of naval ratings was authorized. The ships were to observe and report by radio Japanese movements to the West China Sea and Gulf of Siam. The President prescribed the point at which each vessel was to be stationed. One vessel was to be stationed between Hainan and Hue, one between Camranh Bay and Cape St Jaques, and one off Pointe De Camau. All these points were clearly in the path of the Japanese advance down the coast of Indo-China, and toward the Gulf of Siam. The Navy Department did not originate this plan. The Navy Department would not have directed it to be done unless the President had specifically ordered it.

Admiral Hart was already conducting reconnaissance off that coast by planes from Manila. So far as the Navy Department was concerned, sufficient information was being received from this air reconnaissance. Had the Japanese fired upon any one of these three small vessels, it would have constituted an overt act on the part of Japan. Interferences such as these by superior officers, however, permitted by the line of authority, breed indifference to responsibility on the part of the officer who is superseded.

In the early morning of December 7, 1941, about 5 a.m. Washington time, the message fixing the hour for delivery of the Japanese note as 1 p.m. Washington time, was available in the Navy Department in Washington. This was 8½ hours before the attack on Pearl Harbor. Admiral Stark and his principal subordinates have testified before us that they had knowledge of this message about 10:30 a.m. This was 5½ hours after it had been received in the Navy Department. It was about 3 hours before the attack.

The relation of 1 p.m. Washington time to early morning in Hawaii was pointed out to Admiral Stark. It meant dawn in Hawaii—the strategic time at which to launch an attack. Admiral Stark was urged by the Director of Naval Intelligence to send a warning to the fleet. The chief intelligence officers of the Army had the "1 p.m. message" by 9 a.m. Washington time, immediately appreciated its significance, but did not succeed in bringing it to General Marshall's attention until nearly several hours later. Marshall was horseback riding in Virginia. No action was taken by the Army until he saw and read the 1 p.m. message and related intercepts, at which time he sent a message to General Short which went over commercial facilities and was received after the Pearl Harbor attack. Admiral Stark took no action on this information except to agree to the inclusion in the belated Army message of instructions to General Short to advise Admiral Kimmel of its contents.

Mr Hull, Mr Stimson, and Mr Knox had the 1 p.m. message at their conference about 10:30 a.m. Washington time, December 7. The relation of Washington time to time in Hawaii and the Philippines was brought to their attention. Mr Stimson's notes describing the Sunday morning conference state:

> Today is the day that the Japanese are going to bring their answer to Hull and everything in "Magic" indicated they had been keeping the time back until now in order to accomplish something hanging in the air. Knox and I arranged conference with Hull at 10:30 and we talked the whole matter over. Hull very certain that the Japs are planning some deviltry and we are all wondering where the blow will strike.

On the morning of December 7, before 8 o'clock, Navy Intelligence had ready for high authorities of the United States Government a translation of its intercept of the fourteenth and final part of the Japanese memorandum.

The fact that General Marshall decided on the basis of the intercepts of Japanese messages made available on or before 11:25 on the morning of December 7, to send an urgent war warning to the outpost commanders is itself evidence that, despite previous messages to outpost commanders, Washington authorities recognized that their knowledge of these intercepts and their minute direction of affairs placed an obligation on them to convey precise information to outpost commanders and to make sure that they were on an all-out alert for war. Owing to inexcusable delays in Washington, this final warning to General Short did not reach him until after the Japanese attack.

General Marshall failed to use the scrambler telephone on his desk to call General Short in Hawaii on Sunday morning, December 7, nearly two hours before the attack, and give him the same information which he sent in the delayed telegram which reached General Short after the attack. General Marshall testified that among the possible factors which may have influenced him against using the scrambler telephone was the possibility that the Japanese could construe the fact that the Army was alerting its garrisons in Hawaii as a hostile act:

> The Japanese would have grasped at most any straw to bring to such portions of our public that doubted our integrity of action that we were committing an act that forced action on their part.

This explanation is no excuse for the failure to put the Hawaiian commanders on the full alert for defense. Such an alert could not be considered a hostile or aggressive act on the part of the United States.

The decision of the President, in view of the Constitution, to await the Japanese attack rather than ask for a declaration of war by Congress, increased the responsibility of high authorities in Washington to use the utmost care in putting the commanders at Pearl Harbor on a full alert for defensive actions before the Japanese attack on December 7, 1941.

The difficulty of coping effectively with the menace of Japanese hostilities by the method of maneuvering and waiting for an attack or attacks (conclusions 2, 3, and 4) was recognized by the President and his immediate subordinates. They knew that the power to declare war was vested in Congress alone by the Constitution. Prime Minister Churchill, who had referred to this matter at the Atlantic Conference, again suggested to President Roosevelt, on November 30, 1941, that the President inform the Japanese that further aggression on their part would compel him "to place the gravest issues before Congress." President Roosevelt must have given serious thought to the constitutional difficulty during the several days prior to December 7, while he was considering plans for a special message to Congress.

After it was decided, therefore, that no message be sent to Congress it then became all the more incumbent upon the President and the Secretary of War, the Secretary of the Navy, the Chief of Staff, and the Chief of Naval Operations to make doubly certain that war warning messages to General Short and Admiral Kimmel be so clearly formulated as to mean to them an all-out alert of the forces under their command.

Inasmuch as the knowledge respecting Japanese designs and operations which was in the possession of high authorities in Washington differed in nature and volume from that in the possession of the Pearl Harbor commanders, it was especially incumbent upon the former to formulate instructions to the latter in language not open to misinterpretations as to the obligations imposed on the commanders by the instructions.

Since Washington authorities knew that vital information in their possession—diplomatic, military, and naval—was not being sent to General Short and Admiral Kimmel, and that this was because of Washington's own decision, it was obligatory for them to give particular care to the formulation of messages to the commanders which revealed the growing war tension, the menacing imminence of the breach in American–Japanese relations, and the resolve of those high authorities to wait for an attack, while still carrying on maneuvering.

The increasing assumption of the detailed direction of affairs by high authorities in Washington added to the obligation of those high authorities to give precise instructions to the outpost commanders.

For information in possession of Washington authorities not sent to General Short and Admiral Kimmel, see Army Pearl Harbor Board and Navy Pearl Harbor Court of Inquiry reports, top secret reports, and top secret memoranda. It is true that General Short and Admiral Kimmel had a great deal of information as to Japanese designs and operations which was not in the messages sent to them by the War Department and the Navy Department. It is also true that there were differences of opinion among high authorities in Washington over the nature of the information conveyed by certain intercepts; for example, the so-called "winds message" and the activating "winds message." But it is beyond all question that Washington authorities had a large volume of information, particularly as to vital diplomatic decisions and Japanese intentions, which was not transmitted to the Hawaiian commanders. This withholding of information from General Short and Admiral Kimmel was in part due to general policy adopted in Washington.

General Sherman Miles, at the hearing of November 30, testified that neither the intercepted messages nor essential information derived from them had been sent to Hawaii, although in exceptional cases the substance of some messages had been transmitted in naval code. The exceptional practice of sending the substance in some messages was stopped in July 1941 and General Miles testified that, so far as he knew, General Short and Admiral Kimmel were not notified of this change—this discontinuance of sending even the substance of some intercepts.

Admiral Kimmel had requested all information and was assured by Admiral Stark he would get it. A few messages were sent up until December 7, but he had no notice that he was not getting all the information available.

From among the numerous items of crucial information in possession of Navy Intelligence and Washington authorities and not transmitted to General Short, one may be selected as particularly pertinent to Pearl Harbor. Through its intelligence sources in the Fourteenth Naval District at Pearl Harbor and in Washington, the Navy discovered the presence at Jaluit, in the Marshall Islands, of a Japanese fleet composed of aircraft carriers and other vessels, but lost track of it about December 1. Jaluit is 1,500 miles nearer to Pearl Harbor than is the mainland of Japan. The Japanese fleet there was a strong force capable of attacking Hawaii. Information about this Japanese fleet was delivered to the War Department, but it was not transmitted to General Short. General Short testified during the Army Board hearings on Pearl Harbor that knowledge of the Japanese fleet at Jaluit would have materially modified his point of view and actions.

Japan had fixed a dead-line date of November 25 extended to November 29 for reaching a diplomatic agreement with the United States. There were at least six Japanese messages. If the dead-line date passed without agreement, the Japanese Government advised her ambassadors in Washington: "Things are automatically going to happen." The necessity for agreement by the dead-line date was stressed by Japan in these terms: "The fate of our Empire hangs by the slender thread of a few days; and also we gambled the fate of our land on the throw of this die."

On November 26, 1941, prior to the advanced "dead-line" date, the United States Government delivered to Japan a diplomatic note which the intercepted messages revealed Japan considered to be a "humiliating proposal," impossible of acceptance. The intercepted diplomatic messages further revealed that Japan expected to "rupture" negotiations with the United States when she replied to the American note of November 26. To prevent the United States from becoming unduly suspicious Japan instructed her envoys in Washington to keep up a pretext of continuing negotiations until this Japanese reply was ready for delivery.

A message from the Japanese Government to its ambassador in Berlin, sent on November 30, was intercepted and translated to the Navy in Washington on December 1. In this message the Japanese Ambassador was instructed to:

> immediately interview Chancellor Hitler and Foreign
> Minister Ribbentrop and confidentially communicate to
> them a summary of development. Say very secretly to
> them that there is extreme danger that war may suddenly
> break out between the Anglo-Saxon nations and Japan
> through some clash of arms and add the time of the
> breaking out of this war may come quicker than anyone
> dreams.

The President regarded this message as of such interest that he retained a copy of it, contrary to the usual practice in handling the intercepted messages.

On December 2, 1941, elaborate instructions from Japan were intercepted dealing in precise detail with the method of internment of American and British nationals in Asia "on the outbreak of war with England and the United States." None of these messages showing the imminence of war was sent to Admiral Kimmel or General Short.

Conflicting messages to Hawaiian commanders

The messages sent to General Short and Admiral Kimmel by high authorities in Washington during November were couched in such conflicting and imprecise language that they failed to convey to the commanders definite information on the state of diplomatic relations with Japan and on Japanese war designs and positive orders respecting the particular actions to be taken—orders that were beyond all reasonable doubts as to the need for an all-out alert. In this regard the said high authorities failed to discharge their full duty.

On this subject the Committee has before it hundreds of pages of testimony, exhibits, and documents in which conflicting views are expressed by men presumably of competence and understanding as to the sufficiency or insufficiency of the war warnings to General Short and Admiral Kimmel. According to the obligations conferred upon the Committee by the joint resolution creating it, as explained by Senator Barkley in his address to the Senate on September 6, 1945, the Committee is bound to weigh all messages and information available to General Short and Admiral Kimmel.

A full review of all the testimony, exhibits, and papers relative to the so-called war-warning messages sent to General Short and Admiral Kimmel would fill a volume of at least 500 pages, so we content ourselves with presenting the following facts in respect to the conflicting, imprecise, and insufficient character of these messages.

It should be here observed that Washington had taken unto itself such a minute direction of affairs as regards outposts that the usual discretion of outpost commanders was narrowly limited.

First of all, it is to be noted that the four reports by the Army and Navy Boards created to investigate Pearl Harbor found the warning messages insufficient to put the Hawaiian commanders on a full war alert; and the President's Commission on Pearl Harbor, while finding the commanders guilty of dereliction of duty, itself places neglect on the part of the War Department, in respect to such orders, as among the contributory causes of the catastrophe at Pearl Harbor; thus qualifying its own conclusions.

The President's Commission, though limited by his instructions to a search for derelictions of duty and errors of judgment on the part of the Army and Navy personnel, made a point of declaring that the Secretary of State, the Secretary of War, and the Secretary of the Navy had fulfilled their obligations with regard to matters bearing in the situation at Pearl Harbor and that the Chief of Staff and the Chief of Naval Operations had fulfilled their command responsibilities in issuing warning messages to the two commanders.

But the Commission includes among the grounds for charging General Short and Admiral Kimmel with dereliction of duty their failure "to consult and confer" with each other "respecting the meaning and intent of the warnings." Thus the Commission in effect concedes that the war warning messages were couched in language so imprecise that the commanders would have to consult and confer in order to discover what the messages meant.

Having made this statement, the Commission goes on to lay some of the blame for the Pearl Harbor catastrophe on the War Department and the Navy Department (that is, upon Secretary Stimson, Secretary Knox, and/or General Marshall and Admiral Stark, whom the Commission had earlier in its report exculpated). The Commission declared that among the causes contributory to the success of the Japanese attack were:

> Emphasis in the warning messages on the probability of aggressive Japanese action in the Far East and on anti-sabotage measures. Failure of the War Department to reply to the message relating to the anti-sabotage measures instituted by the commanding general Hawaiian Department.

Had the Commission been in a mind to do so, it might have added: Failure of the War and Navy Departments to mention in these messages the probability of an attack on Pearl Harbor.

Secretary Stimson apparently was not considering the attack at Pearl Harbor when the message of November 27 was prepared, for he said: "The main question has been over the message that we shall send to MacArthur." General MacArthur, having the "Magic" intercepts, was in a better position to judge the situation than was Admiral Kimmel who had to rely upon the inadequate and ambiguous information from Washington.

Finally, it is to be noted that the Commission also places among the "contributory causes" the "non-receipt by the interested parties, prior to the attack, of the warning message of December 7, 1941." As a matter of fact the "non-receipt" of this warning message was due to inexcusable delays of high authorities in Washington.

Hence, it appears that the President's Commission, by direct statements and by implication, admits definitely that the war-warning messages to General Short and Admiral Kimmel were imprecise, indefinite, and constituted no sufficient warning for an all-out alert, particularly the messages to General Short, whose primary duty it was to defend Pearl Harbor and protect the fleet while in the harbor.

The Army Pearl Harbor Board, after a careful examination and comparison of the war-warning messages, concluded that the messages of November 27 were "conflicting" and that the statements in the message to General Short were "inadequate" and "misleading." The Army Board also criticized the War Department for failure to send "specific directives" to outpost commanders.

Despite its conclusion that General Short had displayed lack of judgment, the Army Board laid against him no charge of dereliction of duty and made no recommendations in that respect. The Navy Court of Inquiry likewise criticized the war-warning messages for lack of directives as to actions at Pearl Harbor and concluded that "no offenses have been committed nor serious blame incurred on the part of any person or persons in the naval service." It recommended no further proceedings be had in the matter.

In the testimony and other evidence presented to this Committee there is no proof that warrants traversing the judgment reached by the President's Commission, the Army Pearl Harbor Board, or the Navy Pearl Harbor Court to the effect that the war-warning messages were not in fact clear and unmistakable directives for an all-out alert against a probable Japanese attack on Pearl Harbor. The fundamental messages in the nature of "war warnings" were those of November 24 and 27.

On November 24, 1941, Admiral Kimmel received the following message marked for action:

CHANCES OF FAVORABLE OUTCOME OF NEGOTIATIONS WITH
JAPAN VERY DOUBTFUL. THIS SITUATION COUPLED WITH

STATEMENTS OF JAPANESE GOVERNMENT AND MOVEMENTS
THEIR NAVAL AND MILITARY FORCES INDICATE IN OUR OPINION
THAT A SURPRISE AGGRESSIVE MOVEMENT IN ANY DIRECTION
INCLUDING ATTACK ON PHILIPPINES OR GUAM IS A POSSIBILITY.
CHIEF OF STAFF HAS SEEN THIS DISPATCH CONCURS AND
REQUESTS ACTION ADEES TO INFORM SENIOR ARMY OFFICERS
THEIR AREAS. UTMOST SECRECY NECESSARY IN ORDER NOT TO
COMPLICATE AN ALREADY TENSE SITUATION OR PRECIPITATE
JAPANESE ACTION. GUAM WILL BE INFORMED SEPARATELY

On the next day, November 25, Admiral Stark confused the directions in this message and diluted its
effectiveness by sending a letter to Admiral Kimmel in
which Admiral Stark concluded: "I won't go into the pros
and cons of what the United States may do. I'll be damned
if I know. I wish I did." The postscript of this letter read:

I held this up pending a meeting with the President and
Mr Hull today. Have been in constant touch with Mr
Hull and it was only after a long talk with him that I sent
the message to you a day or two ago showing the gravity
of the situation. He confirmed it all in today's meeting, as
did the President. Neither would be surprised over a
Japanese surprise attack. From any angles an attack on the
Philippines would be the most embarrassing thing that
could happen to us. There are some here who think it
likely to occur. I do not give it the weight others do, but
I included it because of the strong feeling among some
people. You know I have generally held that it was not
time for the Japanese to proceed against Russia. I still do.
Also I still rather look for an advance into Thailand, Indo-
China, Burma Road areas as the most likely.

I won't go into the pros or cons of what the United
States may do. I will be damned if I know. I wish I did. The
only thing I do know is that we may do most anything and

that's the only thing I know to be prepared for; or we may
do nothing—I think it is more likely to be "anything."

If any candid person has doubt about their insufficiency to
constitute orders for an all-out alert to meet a probable
Japanese attack on Pearl Harbor, he can allay his doubt by
examining carefully the messages of November 27 to
General Short and Admiral Kimmel printed below.

To General Short
Negotiations with Japanese appear to be terminated to all
practical purposes with only the barest possibilities that the
Japanese Government might come back and offer to
continue. Japanese future action unpredictable but hostile
action possible at any moment. If hostilities cannot, repeat
cannot, be avoided the US desires that Japan commit the
first overt act. This policy should not, repeat not, be
construed as restricting you to a course of action as might
jeopardize your defense. Prior to Japanese hostile action
you are directed to undertake such reconnaissance and
other measures as you deem necessary but these measures
should be carried out so as not, repeat not, to alarm the
civil population or disclose intent. Report measures taken.
Should hostilities occur, you will carry out tasks assigned
in Rainbow Five as far as they pertain to Japan. Limit
dissemination of this highly secret information to
minimum essential officers.

To Admiral Kimmel
Consider this dispatch a war warning. The negotiations
with Japan in an effort to stabilize conditions in the Pacific
have ended. Japan is expected to make aggressive move
within the next few days. An amphibious expedition
against either the Philippines, Thai, or Kra Peninsula or
possibly Borneo is indicated by the number and

equipment of Japanese troops and the organization of their naval task forces. You will execute a defensive deployment in preparation for carrying out the tasks assigned in WPL-46 only. [WPL-46 was an over-all plan of action to be placed in effect by United States forces, in association with the British and Dutch, when war finally broke out.] Guam, Samoa, and Continental Districts have been directed to take appropriate measures against sabotage. A similar warning is being sent by the War Department. Inform naval district and Army authorities. British to be informed by Spenavo.

Admiral Kimmel also received several messages assigning his carriers to the movement of planes to other islands.

The use of the term "war warning" in constant reference to this message of November 27 to Admiral Kimmel creates a wrong impression. The entire message is of the utmost importance and should be read as a whole rather than adopt two words from it which when taken alone create the wrong impression.

In response to the message to him, General Short soon replied that he had alerted his command against sabotage. The Chief of the War Plans Division of the Army, General Leonard T. Gerow, saw General Short's reply, noted and initialed it. General Marshall saw General Short's reply, initialed the document to which it was appended, and routed it to the Secretary of War. The Secretary of War saw, noted, and initialed General Short's reply.

General Marshall had in May 1941 taken with him to the President an aide memoire concerning the defense of Hawaii. It contained the following sentence:

In point of sequence sabotage is first to be expected and may within a very limited time cause great damage. On this account and in order to assure strong control, it would be highly desirable to set up a military control of the islands prior to the likelihood of our involvement in the Far East.

To General Short's response, the War Department made no answer whatever. The President's Commission on Pearl Harbor took note of this failure on the part of the War Department and placed it among the contributory causes of the catastrophe. In their testimony before this Committee, General Marshall and General Gerow admitted that the failure to inform General Short immediately as to the insufficiency of his anti-sabotage alert was a mistake on their part and General Marshall took full responsibility upon himself for this failure. Reasonably conclusive evidence that the war warning messages which had been sent to General Short and Admiral Kimmel on November 27 were insufficient to constitute a proper and adequate war warning is provided by General Marshall's decision to send another warning message to General Short on the morning of December 7, despite the insistence of other high authorities in Washington that the previous messages were sufficient.

Two points in the message of November 27 to General Short deserve special consideration. It informed him that "the United States desires Japan to commit the first overt act," if hostilities cannot be avoided. And it also informed him that such measures as he deemed necessary to adopt "should be carried out so as not to alarm the civil population or disclose intent." A limitation on dissemination was to "minimum essential officers."

As to "overt act," it is to be emphasized that an all-out alert for defense against a possible or probable attack

by an enemy is not an overt act of war. Nor did the
Government of the United States regard it as such, for, on
the basis of reports respecting a probable Japanese attack,
General Marshall, on June 17, 1940, instructed General
Herron, the commanding general in Hawaii, to order an
all-out, full, war alert and the armed forces were set in
motion immediately and kept alerted for six weeks. This
message reads:

> Immediately alert complete defense organization to deal
> with possible trans-Pacific raid comma to greatest extent
> possible without creating public hysteria or provoking
> undue curiosity of newspapers or alien agents. Suggest
> maneuver basis. Maintain alert until further orders.
> Instructions for secret communication direct with Chief of
> Staff will be furnished you shortly. Acknowledge.

No United States official then regarded this action as an
overt act against Japan. Moreover, when in this 1940 case
Washington authorities were worried about hostile
Japanese action, they ordered the commanding general at
Hawaii in language that was crystal clear.

The fact is that the War Department and Navy
Department did not instruct General Short and Admiral
Kimmel to put into effect an all-out war alert, and the War
Department was informed by General Short that he had
actually put into effect the alert against sabotage.
Furthermore, the actions of the War Department in
instructing General Short in November and December, as
the Army Pearl Harbor Board correctly stated, showed "a
lack of adequate procedure under which to advise the
Hawaiian Department and to control its actions."

The War Department failed to reply to General Short's
anti-sabotage report. It failed to give him further instructions for a stronger alert. These failures, it is reasonable to

say, contributed heavily to the unpreparedness existing at Pearl Harbor when the Japanese struck.

It could reasonably follow from this failure that the Army airplanes, instead of being scattered, were bunched together wing to wing; ammunition, except that near the fixed antiaircraft guns, was in storehouses; antiaircraft artillery and two combat divisions were in their permanent quarters and not in combat positions. As the Army Pearl Harbor Board stated: "Everything was concentrated in close confines by reason of the anti-sabotage alert No. 1. This made them easy targets for an air attack."

In short, everything that was done made the situation perfect for an air attack, and the Japanese took full advantage of it. This was known to the War Department by General Short's reply to the message of November 27, but the Department took no action. The President's lack of power under the Constitution to meet the Japanese menace by an attack without a declaration of war by Congress increased the responsibility of high authorities in Washington to use the utmost care in putting the commanders at Pearl Harbor on full alert for defensive actions before the Japanese attack on December 7, 1941. This they did not do.

Failure and negligence of the President and Washington authorities

High authorities in Washington failed in giving proper weight to the evidence before them respecting Japanese designs and operations which indicated that an attack on Pearl Harbor was highly probable, and they failed also to emphasize this probability in messages to the Hawaiian commanders. The following passage in the war-warning message of November 27 from the Navy Department to Admiral Kimmel reflected the loose thinking that prevailed widely in Washington:

Japan is expected to make an aggressive move within the next few days. An amphibious expedition against either the Philippines, Thai, or Kra Peninsula, or possibly Borneo, is indicated by the number and equipment of Japanese troops and by the organization of their naval forces.

These words not only displayed the apparent ignorance of Washington authorities respecting Japanese designs on Pearl Harbor but also gratuitously conveyed to Admiral Kimmel a false impression. Although the message of the War Department to General Short on the same day did not contain these misleading words, General Short, in conferring with Admiral Kimmel on "the meaning and intent" of their messages learned about this expectation that the Japanese attack would occur in the Far East.

The failure of Washington authorities to act promptly and consistently in translating intercepts, evaluating information, and sending appropriate instructions to the Hawaiian commanders was in considerable measure due to delays, mismanagement, non-cooperation, unpreparedness, confusion, and negligence on the part of officers in Washington.

As to delays, take for example section 13 of Japanese Messages Concerning Military Installations, Ship Movements, Etc. Pages 16–29 give "messages translated after December 7, 1941." Here are messages exchanged by the Japanese Government and its agents. Meanwhile we are exchanging views with the British Government in regard to the entire situation and the tremendous problems which are presented, with a view to effective coordinating of efforts in the most practicable way possible.

Indirectly influencing that situation: American military and naval defensive forces on the Philippine Islands,

which are being steadily increased, and the United States
Fleet at Hawaii, lying as they do along the flank of any
Japanese military movement into China from Indo-China,
are ever present and significant factors in the whole situation, as are the increasing British and Dutch defensive
preparations in their territories to the south (State
Department message, approved by President Roosevelt
and transmitted through Ambassador Hu Shih to Chiang
Kai-shek) which were intercepted by American intelligence services before December 7, but not translated until
after December 7. Special attention should be drawn to
the message from a Japanese agent in Honolulu to Tokyo
on December 6, 1941, listing the ships at anchor in Pearl
Harbor on that day and reporting to Tokyo: "It appears that
no air reconnaissance is being conducted by the fleet air
arm"—a fact with which high authorities in Washington
were not acquainted, if the testimony before this
Committee is accepted as accurate and comprehensive.

One of the great tragedies was that a message sent
from Honolulu to Tokyo on December 6, 1941, was not
translated until December 8, 1941, after the attack. The following appeared in the message: "at the present time there
are no signs of barrage balloon equipment. I imagine that
in all probability there is considerable opportunity left to
take advantage for a surprise attack against these places."

Another message intercepted and translated in the
rough and available on the desk of a responsible officer in
the Naval Intelligence on the afternoon of December 6,
1941, provided for land–sea signals at Hawaii. These signals
were intended to disclose to the Japanese the location of
our ships in Pearl Harbor—apparently nothing was done
about the message either in evaluating it in Washington or
transmitting it to the commanders in Hawaii.

Since President Roosevelt was convinced as early as the middle of August that a clash with Japan was a matter of a few weeks, the responsible officers of his administration had ample time to strengthen, organize, and consolidate the agencies in Washington, especially the Army and Navy communication and intelligence services, in such a manner to assure the speedy translations of intercepts, prompt distribution to the appropriate officials, swift evaluation, and proper decisions based on such information and evaluation. Lack of time cannot be pleaded as an excuse for this failure, despite the difficulties involved in securing competent and reliable specialists.

General Miles admitted at the hearing on December 3, 1945, that there had been no meeting of the joint Army–Navy Intelligence Committee between October 11 and December 8 or 9, 1941, and declared:

> I regret to say, Mr Congressman there were still discussions and difficulties going on between the War and Navy Departments as to just what the functions of that committee would be, where it would sit, what rooms it would have, what secretary it would be allowed, etcetera.

There was lack of cooperation between the Army and the Navy regarding the 14 parts of the Japanese final message between 9:30 p.m. on December 6 and the morning of December 7 about 10:30. The existence of the first 13 parts of this Japanese message, which President Roosevelt received between 9 and 10 o'clock on Saturday evening and interpreted as meaning war, was known more or less accidentally to certain high Army and Navy authorities about the same time. But Admiral Stark testified before this Committee at the hearing on January 1, 1946, that the first 13 parts and the directive for delivery to Secretary Hull at one o'clock Sunday, did not come to his attention until late on the morning of December 7. Admiral Stark thought that he went to his office between 10:30 and 11 o'clock that morning and that as nearly as he could remember he did not see the directive message for one o'clock delivery until about 10:40 that morning. It was the final part of the Japanese message, and the one o'clock directive that convinced General Marshall that war was immediately at hand and led him to send the warning dispatch which reached General Short after the Japanese attack.

For this non-cooperation and mismanagement, high authorities in Washington were fully responsible. The President, the Secretary of State, the Secretary of War, the Secretary of the Navy, General Marshall, and Admiral Stark were all in Washington or environs. It is true that General Marshall and Admiral Stark—when they appeared before this Committee—could not remember where they were during the evening and night of December 6 but they were at least accessible to officers of the Army and Navy Departments, or should have been; hence, there was no excuse for the failure of these high authorities to assemble on the evening of December 6, inquire into the defensive preparedness of outpost commanders, and send peremptory directives to them.

The setting up of so many councils and committees, and the intermeddling of so many men, created such a state of confusion in Washington that the high principle of individual responsibility was apparently lost to sight. The result was that no one among the President's chief subordinates was enough concerned on the night of December 6 to do anything about the 13 parts which indicated a crucial stage in Japanese–American relations.

In the lower, operating echelons of the Army and Navy, on the other hand, men seemed to see or to sense the gathering crisis and even the immediate danger to

Hawaii. They tried to take steps to meet it but were discouraged by their superiors. This was notably evident in the testimony of Captain Arthur McCollum, Chief of the Far Eastern Section of Naval Intelligence. Alarmed by conditions on December 4, 1941, he prepared a dispatch to fully alert the fleets in the Pacific. He tried to get permission to send this dispatch at a meeting attended by Admiral Stark, Ingersoll, Turner, and Wilkinson but was discouraged from doing so on the ground that the messages of November 24 and 27 to Admiral Kimmel were sufficient. He protested that it was not sufficient and that he would like to send his December 4 dispatch anyway. The dispatch he prepared and wanted to send was never sent, and the result was tragic.

Finally, there is no excuse for the failure of General Marshall and Admiral Stark to be on the alert early Sunday morning or for their failure, after they did meet near the middle of the morning, to reach the outpost commanders with a definite war-warning message before the Japanese attack came at Pearl Harbor. This failure was all the more inexcusable for the reason that some time in July 1941, the practice of sending intercepts to General Short and Admiral Kimmel had been abandoned.

The President of the United States was responsible for the failure to enforce continuous, efficient, and appropriate cooperation among the Secretary of War, the Secretary of the Navy, the Chief of Staff, and the Chief of Naval Operations, in evaluating information and dispatching clear and positive orders to the Hawaiian commanders as events indicated the growing imminence of war; for the Constitution and laws of the United States vested in the President full power, as Chief Executive and Commander in Chief, to compel such cooperation and vested this power in him alone with a view to establishing his responsibility to the people of the United States.

As to the power, and therefore of necessity, the responsibility of the President in relation to the chain of events leading to the catastrophe at Pearl Harbor, there can be no doubt. The terms of the Constitution and the laws in this respect are clear beyond all cavil. The Constitution vests in the President the whole and indivisible executive power subject to provisions for the approval of appointments and treaties by the Senate. The President, by and with the advice and consent of the Senate, appoints high officers, civil and military. He is Chief Magistrate in all civil affairs, including those related to the maintenance and operation of the Military and Naval Establishments. Under the law he conducts all diplomatic negotiations on behalf the United States, assigning to his appointee, the Secretary of State, such duties connected therewith as he sees fit, always subject to his own instructions and authorizations.

Under the Constitution the President is Commander in Chief of the armed forces of the United States, and with the approval of the Senate he appoints all high military and naval officers. He assigns them to their duties in his discretion except in the case of the Chief of Staff and Chief of Naval Operations—these appointments must be approved by the Senate.

The framers of the Constitution vested these immense powers in one magistrate to assure "energy in the Executive," "a due dependence to the people," and "a due responsibility." A plural Executive, it is there argued, "tends to deprive the people of the two greatest securities they can have for the faithful exercise of any delegated power, first, the restraints of public opinion; and, secondly, the opportunity of discovering with facility and clearness the misconduct of persons they trust."

The acts of Congress providing for the organization, operations, powers, and duties of the Military Establishments under the President particularized the powers and duties of the President in relation to them; in brief, they empowered him to issue orders and instructions to the civil Secretaries and also directly to the Chief of Staff and the Chief of Naval Operations.

Such are the terms of the Constitution and the laws relative to the Chief Executive.

From March 4, 1933, to December 7, 1941, Franklin D. Roosevelt was President and Commander in Chief of the armed forces of the United States and in him was vested all Executive powers under the Constitution and the laws.

He appointed Cordell Hull as Secretary of State in 1933 and retained him in that office during this period. He appointed all the Secretaries of War and of the Navy during this period. He selected, or approved the choice of, all Chiefs of Staff and Chiefs of Naval Operations during this period. He selected, or approved the choice of, all the men who served as military and naval commanders in charge of the Hawaiian area and he assigned them to their posts of duty.

In support of the doctrine that the President is entrusted with supreme Executive responsibility and cannot divest himself of it, we have more recent authority. Speaking at a press conference on December 20, 1940, on a subject of administrative actions, President Roosevelt said: "There were two or three cardinal principles; and one of them is the fact that you cannot, under the Constitution, set up a second President of the United States. In other words, the Constitution states one man is responsible. Now that man can delegate, surely, but in the delegation he does not delegate away any part of the responsibility from the ultimate responsibility that rests on him."

Although there were two departments for the administration of military and naval affairs during this period,
they were both under the supreme direction of the
President as Chief Executive and Commander in Chief in
all matters relative to separate and joint planning of
defense and war, to disposition of forces and materiel, to
preparedness for operation in case of an attack. In respect
of the President's power, the two departments were one
agency for over-all planning and operational purposes.

The President had power to issue directions and
orders to the Secretary of War and the Secretary of the
Navy and also directly and indirectly to the Chief of Staff
and the Chief of Naval Operations and on occasions used
this power.

Furthermore, under the Reorganization Act of 1939,
President Roosevelt had enjoyed the power, by grant of
Congress, to reorganize the Department of War and the
Department of the Navy if he deemed it necessary in the
interest of efficiency and more effective cooperation
between the Departments. Since he did not reorganize the
two Departments under that act, he must have deemed
them properly constructed as they were.

By virtue of the powers vested in him the President
had, during this period, the responsibility for determining
the reciprocal relations of diplomatic decisions and war
plans.

In fine, Secretary Hull, Secretary Stimson, Secretary
Knox, General Marshall, Admiral Stark, General Short, and
Admiral Kimmel were all men of President Roosevelt's
own choice—not hang-over appointees from another
administration to which incompetence may be ascribed—
and the President had ample power to direct them,
coordinate their activities, and bring about a concentration
of their talents and energies in the defense of the United
States.

Thus endowed with power and in full charge of diplomatic negotiations, the President decided long before December 7, at least as early as the Atlantic Conference in August, that war with Japan was a matter of a few weeks or months, was so highly probable and so imminent as to warrant a dedication of his abilities to preparation for that war. Having decided against an appeal to Congress for a declaration of war and having resolved that he would avoid even the appearance of an overt act against Japan, the President chose the alternative of waiting for an overt act by Japan—an attack on territory of the United States. Possessing full power to prepare for meeting such an attack and for countering it with the armed forces under his command, he had supreme responsibility for making sure that the measures, plans, orders, and dispositions necessary to that end were taken.

During the weeks and days preceding the Japanese attack on December 7, 1941, the President and his chief subordinates held many meetings, discussed the practical certainty of an attack, and, jointly or severally, made decisions and plans in relation to the coming of that attack—or overt act. Yet when the Japanese attack came at Pearl Harbor the armed forces of the United States failed to cope with the attack effectively.

In view of all the evidence cited in support of the preceding conclusions, and more of the same kind that could be cited, this failure cannot all be ascribed to General Short and Admiral Kimmel, nor to their immediate superiors, civil and military. Those authorities had their powers and corresponding responsibilities but the ultimate power and responsibility under the Constitution and the laws were vested in the President of the United States.

This does demonstrate the weakness of dependence on the political head of the Government to bring about the necessary coordination of the operating activities of the military branches, particularly in the areas of intelligence. The major lesson to be learned is that this coordination should be done in advance of a crisis.

High authorities in Washington failed to allocate to the Hawaiian commanders the materiel which the latter often declared to be necessary to defense and often requested, and no requirements of defense or war in the Atlantic did or could excuse these authorities or their failures in this respect.

The first part of this conclusion calls for no special citations of authority. In reports of the President's Commission, of the Army Pearl Harbor Board, and of the Navy Court of Inquiry, three points in this respect are accepted as plain facts: (1) The ultimate power to allocate arms, ammunition, implements of war, and other supplies was vested in the President and his aide, Harry Hopkins, subject to the advice of General Marshall and Admiral Stark; (2) General Short and Admiral Kimmel made repeated demands upon their respective Departments for additional materiel, which they represented as necessary to the effective defense of Pearl Harbor; and (3) Washington authorities, having full discretion in this regard, made decisions against General Short and Admiral Kimmel and allocated to the Atlantic theater, where the United States was at least nominally at peace, materiel, specially bombing and reconnaissance planes, which were known to be absolutely indispensable to efficient defense of Pearl Harbor.

The decision to base the fleet at Pearl Harbor was made by the President in March 1940, over the protest of Admiral Richardson.

The second part of this conclusion may be arguable from the point of view of some high world strategy, but it is not arguable under the Constitution and laws of the United States. The President it is true had powers and obligations under the Lease-Lend Act of March 1941. But his first and inescapable duty under the Constitution and laws was to care for the defense and security of the United States against a Japanese attack, which he knew was imminent; and, in the allocations of materiel, especially bombing and reconnaissance planes, he made or authorized decisions which deprived the Hawaiian commanders of indispensable materiel they could otherwise have had and thus reduced their defensive forces to a degree known to be dangerous by high officials in Washington and Hawaii.

∞◦◦∞

When this decision to base the fleet at Pearl Harbor was made certain definite facts in relation to such bases must be presumed to have been fully known and appreciated by the responsible command at Washington.

The base is a shallow-water basin with limited base mobility, with no chance for concealment or camouflage and without enough air beaches to properly park the necessary defensive air equipment. Entrance to the base is by a narrow winding channel requiring sorties at reduced speed, and in single file, and presenting the possibility of a blockade of the base by an air or submarine attack on the entrance.

The base is surrounded by high land immediately adjacent to the city of Honolulu, thereby affording full public familiarity with installations and movements within the base at all times.

The base is located on an island where the population was heavily Japanese, and where, as was well known, Japanese espionage was rampant, and making it probable that any defensive insufficiency of any kind or nature would be open to Japanese information.

All of the fuel for the base must be transported, by tanker, from the mainland more than 2,000 miles away, thus intensifying the necessity for complete defensive equipment and supplies for the base.

The waters about Oahu are of a depth facilitating the concealed movement of submarines, and the near approach of submarines to the shore, thereby favoring such methods of hostile attack. The approaches to Oahu cover a full circle of 360 degrees, with open sea available on all sides.

The situation thus confronting the Pacific Fleet upon reaching its Pearl Harbor base seems entirely clear. Before the base could be a safe base, it must be supplied with adequate defense facilities, which facilities must be in kind and amount in relation to the physical characteristics of the base above referred to. An absence of adequate defensive facilities directly increased the peril of the fleet. Since the decision to base the fleet at Pearl Harbor was made at Washington, the responsibility for providing proper base defense for the fleet rested primarily upon Washington. It becomes important, therefore, to consider what defensive equipment was essential to protect the Pearl Harbor base, whether such defensive equipment was supplied, and, if not, the reasons for such failure.

The character of the defensive equipment necessary for the defense of the Pearl Harbor base is not seriously in dispute. Being located on an island, approachable from all directions, the first protective equipment necessary was a sufficient number of long-distance patrol planes to permit proper distance reconnaissance covering a 360-degree perimeter. The evidence indicates that to supply such a reconnaissance program would require approximately 200 patrol planes, with a sufficient supply of spare parts to keep the planes in operation, and a sufficient number of available crews to permit a continuous patrol. Base defense also required sufficient fighter planes to meet any attack which might be considered possible. This would require approximately 175 planes.

The second class of essential defense equipment was a suitable number of antiaircraft batteries with suitable and sufficient ammunition and sufficient experienced crews for ready operation.

The third class of defense equipment were torpedo nets and baffles. It would be necessary for a considerable portion of the fleet to be in Pearl Harbor at all times, fueling and relaxation of men together with ship repairs requiring the ships in the fleet to have constant recourse to the base at more or less regular intervals. The mobility of the Pearl Harbor base was limited, and ships using the base were in a more or less defenseless situation except for the defense power of their own ship batteries. The British attack on the Italian Fleet at Taranto, Italy, brought the question of torpedo bomber defense to the fore. Admiral Stark wrote on November 22, 1940—expressing fear of a "sudden attack in Hawaiian waters" on the fleet, and asking about torpedo net protection. Admiral Richardson, then in command, expressed no anxiety about the security of the fleet, and thought torpedo nets unnecessary, but thought security to the fleet must be carried out, even at the expense of fleet training and extra discomfort. Approximately four-fifths of the damage to the fleet upon the attack was the result of torpedoes fired by torpedo-bombing planes tacking the base at low altitudes. Against such an attack, antitorpedo baffles and nets would have been of extraordinary value.

The fourth class of defense equipment for the base lay in the newly discovered device known as radar, which before December 7 had been sufficiently perfected to permit the discovery of approaching planes more than 100 miles away.

It seems to be agreed that it is not the duty of the fleet, ordinarily, to furnish its own base defense. That duty is supposed to be performed by the base defense itself, usually in the hands of the Army. The fleet, however, is always to be expected to furnish every available defensive effort it has, in event of an attack upon a base. The record discloses that with full knowledge of the defense necessities inherent in the defense of the Pearl Harbor base, and with full knowledge of the dangers and peril imposed upon the fleet while based at the Pearl Harbor base, and with full knowledge of the equipment essential to a proper protection of the fleet at such base, it was decided by President Roosevelt to remove the fleet from the mainland bases and base it at Pearl Harbor.

The record discloses that from the time the fleet arrived at Pearl Harbor until the attack on December 7, the high command at Hawaii, both in the Army and the Navy, frequently advised the military authorities at Washington of the particular defense equipment needs at the Pearl Harbor base. Nowhere in the record does any dissent appear as to the reasonableness, or the propriety, of the requests for defense equipment made by the high command in Hawaii. On the contrary, the necessity for such equipment was expressly recognized and the only explanation given for a failure to provide the equipment was that by reason of unavoidable shortages, the requested defense equipment at Hawaii could not be supplied.

It was asserted that more equipment had been provided for Hawaii than for any other base, and this is probably correct. The trouble with such an explanation is that Hawaii was the only non-mainland base charged with the defense of a major part of our Pacific Fleet, and the equipment supplied to Hawaii was admittedly insufficient. The Philippines received much equipment which might well have gone to Hawaii, because Hawaii could have been defended, whereas no one expected the Philippines to be able to stand a direct Japanese onslaught. General Marshall reported to the President in March 1941 that "Oahu was believed to be the strongest fortress in the world" and practically invulnerable to attack and that sabotage was considered the first danger and might cause great damage.

The Government made the Atlantic theater the primary theater and the Pacific theater a secondary and a defense theater. We raise no issue as to the propriety of such a decision, but we cannot fail to point out that such a decision resulted in the failure of the military authorities in Washington to supply the Pearl Harbor base with military defense equipment which everyone agreed was essential and necessary for the defense of the base and the fleet while in the base. As we have said, such a more or less defenseless condition imposed increased peril upon the Pacific Fleet, so long as it was based at Pearl Harbor. We are forced to conclude, therefore, that in view of the obligations assumed by the Government in other military theaters, and to which we have just referred, and the consequent inability of the Government to properly contribute to the safety of the fleet at Pearl Harbor, that the only alternative left which might have relieved the fleet from the resultant peril would have been to have changed the original decision to base the fleet at Pearl Harbor, and thereupon return the fleet to its several mainland bases.

It appears obvious that the safety of the fleet would have been helped by such removal. The perimeter of a defense at a mainland base would only be 180 degrees instead of 360 degrees, thus permitting distant patrol reconnaissance by one-half as many planes. The transportation and supply facilities to the mainland base would be immensely improved, as would all necessary communication facilities. The mobility of the fleet at a mainland base would have been improved and the concentration of the fleet in a single limited base would have been avoided. We therefore are of the opinion that the fleet should not have been based at Pearl Harbor unless proper base defenses were assured.

Since no such change in policy was approved, and the fleet remained based at Pearl Harbor without the necessary defense equipment to which we have referred—plus the fact that the precise status of the defense weakness must be assumed to have been open to the unusual Japanese espionage operating in Hawaii, and therefore that the Tokyo war office must be assumed to have been cognizant of the status of affairs at Pearl Harbor, we are forced to conclude that the failure to remove the fleet from Pearl Harbor to the mainland must be viewed as an important relevant factor necessarily involved in the success of the Japanese attack on December 7.

The record discloses that the Army and Navy had available, between February 1 and December 1, 1941, an abundance of long-distance patrol planes suitable for reconnaissance purposes. The Army received between February 1 and December 1, 1941, approximately 600 long-distance bombers capable of flying loaded missions of 1,200 miles or more. Of these 12 went to Hawaii and 35 went to the Philippines. During the same period the Navy received approximately 560 similar long-distance bombers, of which approximately 175 were assigned to carriers in the Pacific. During the same period the Army received approximately 5,500 antiaircraft guns, of which seven went to Hawaii and 100 to the Philippines. If it be true that it was found necessary to send this equipment elsewhere, as we assume, still it would seem that Hawaii instead of having high priority, occupied a subordinate position.

We have referred to the unavoidable vulnerabilities of the Pearl Harbor base, together with the identification of the essential defense equipment necessary for its proper defense. We likewise noted the demands made by the high command at Hawaii for such equipment, the agreement that such equipment was proper and necessary, and the continued and increased peril imposed upon the fleet by the failure to provide such equipment.

It seems proper here to note the extent to which the Pearl Harbor base was deprived of needed and essential equipment.

(1) We have pointed out that the perimeter of Oahu defense covered 360 degrees. Full defense reconnaissance would likewise be required for the full 360 degrees. The evidence discloses that it would take approximately 200 patrol planes to furnish such reconnaissance. Such reconnaissance would require flights of not less than 750 miles from Oahu. The evidence shows that the wear and tear upon patrol planes engaged in such distant operations would be heavy, that a certain proportion of available planes would have to be under repair and adjustment, and that only about one-third of the assigned planes would be available for a particular day's patrol. In a similar way, in connection with the overhaul and repair of planes, a

proper store of repair parts would be essential and of even greater importance, spare crews for the operation of the planes would be required, since the same crew could not fly such patrol missions daily.

The record seems to establish that there were available at Pearl Harbor on December 7, approximately 85 patrol planes suitable for distant patrol, of which not to exceed 55 were in operable condition. The supply of spare parts was not ample, nor were there sufficient extra crews for a continuous operation. With reference to fighter planes, the situation was not so acute. An estimate appears in the record that 185 fighter planes would be necessary to defend the base, and there were, on December 7, 105 available fighter planes, which, if properly alerted, would have been available for base defense. The fleet itself had been depleted by assignments to the Atlantic theater, and the man supply for plane service had likewise been used as a reservoir from which to supply reserve demands for that theater.

We agree that Admiral Kimmel was faced with a sharp dilemma. He was the Commander in Chief of the Pacific Fleet. Under WPL-46 he was given specific duties which required him to have his fleet ready for action promptly upon the breaking out of war. He had available 50 or 60 patrol planes, and he would need these planes in aid of fleet movements if his fleet was to take the offensive against the enemy. If he used these patrol planes for base defense, such heavy duty would reduce their efficiency and ultimately put them up for repair in the event the distance patrol duty should cover an extended period. In such an event his fleet could not sail against the enemy as required by WPL-46 because his patrol planes would be out of commission. He had therefore to make a choice between fleet training and preparation and base defense. He says his decision not to carry on distant reconnaissance was based upon his belief, in common with his staff, that Pearl Harbor was not in danger from a Japanese attack. We think the abandonment of distance reconnaissance was unjustified.

(2) The fuel reserves were insufficient, limiting full use of the fleet at sea, required constant augmentation from the mainland, and the location of such fuel supplies was such as to make them vulnerable to any raiding attack. The fleet was required to come into the base at frequent intervals to refuel. The facilities at the base made such refueling slow. The fleet was without a sufficient supply of fast tankers to permit refueling at sea, and there was ever present the inescapable fact that a destruction of the fuel supply would necessarily immobilize the entire fleet.

(3) It is difficult to reach a conclusion with respect to the sufficiency of the antiaircraft batteries and supplies available at Pearl Harbor on December 7. General Short testified as to the number of guns available on December 7, 1941, as compared with the number available in December 1942. It is apparent that the antiaircraft gun equipment had been much augmented during the year following the Pearl Harbor attack.

The difficulty we have with respect to the antiaircraft batteries situation, as with the available force of fighter planes, is that practically none of these guns were alerted on December 7, and ammunition was not readily available, the crews serving them were not in attendance, and the only seeming excuse for such conditions was the common belief that there was no danger of an attack on Pearl Harbor and therefore no reason for any battery alert. Even if there had been twice as many batteries (or fighter planes) available, there is no reason to believe the condition of alert would have been different.

The ships in the harbor were not provided with proper torpedo protection. The letter of June 13, 1941, with respect to the use of aerial torpedoes, seems to demonstrate the responsibility of the high command at Washington to provide a torpedo defense. Such a defense was well known and could have been provided and, if provided, might have obviated the greatest source of damage suffered by the fleet during the raid, even though Admiral Richardson in 1940 thought such defense unnecessary. But it could not have been provided at Hawaii; it had to come from Washington. Washington's advices on the subject did more harm than good, because they intimated that an attack was possible even in shallow water, but at the same time, negatived the probability of attack.

The installation of the radar in Hawaii was inexcusably delayed. It was a method of defense peculiarly essential in Hawaii. It was known that there were insufficient planes and insufficient guns to protect the base, and this made the availability of radar all the more necessary. It seems we could have priority for radar protection in New York and other mainland points, where no attack was probable; but none in Hawaii, where radar information was essential. The result was that fixed radio installations were not accomplished at all prior to the Pearl Harbor attack, and such fixed installations would have furnished the most distant services. The mobile sets available had, by reason of the delay, been operating only on a short experimental basis. There was a scarcity of trained operators. The operators were trying to learn and operate at the same time. The selected hours of operation, which proved of vast importance, were not wisely fixed. Service stopped at 7 a.m., the very time when the danger was acute.

No suitable information center had been established, and it is conceded that such a center was essential to radar information. This was particularly true at Hawaii, because radar had not yet been developed to the point where the nationality of approaching planes could be ascertained. The information as to whether approaching planes were, therefore, friendly or enemy, depended upon the constant presence at an information center of representatives of the military services who could instantly advise as to location of friendly planes. No such information center was established, and no assignment of trained operators to such stations was ever made. Thus, there was no one on duty who could have known whether the approaching planes were enemy planes, or, instead, our own B-17s, en route from the mainland.

Interdependent responsibilities of Washington and Hawaii

The defense of Hawaii rested upon two sets of interdependent responsibilities: (1) The responsibility in Washington in respect of its intimate knowledge of diplomatic negotiations, widespread intelligence information, direction of affairs, and constitutional duty to plan the defense of the United States; (2) the responsibility cast upon the commanders in the field in charge of a major naval base and the fleet essential to the defense of the territory of the United States to do those things appropriate to the defense of the fleet and outpost.

Washington authorities failed in (1) and the commanding officers of Hawaii failed in (2).

In the discharge of these responsibilities neither the high authorities in Washington nor the commanders in Hawaii acted upon the assumption or belief that Hawaii could or would be the point of any hostile attack. Therefore, in discharging their respective responsibilities neither the Washington authorities nor the field commanders interpreted those responsibilities in the terms of danger to Hawaii. Many of the failures of performance can be attributed to this cardinal fact.

Evidence set forth in this report in detail is ample to show that in the period approximately from May 1940 to

December 7, 1941, the high authorities at Washington assumed so much of the direction of affairs at Hawaii as to remove many of the basic responsibilities from the commanders in the field. The result was to reduce the discretion of the commanders in the field by those things which they were ordered to do by directions from Washington and not to do certain things unless they were so ordered from Washington. Another result of this practice was to lull the commanders in the field into awaiting instructions from Washington.

Being charged with the responsibility attaching to the highest command in Washington and having taken so much of the responsibility and direction of affairs away from the commanders in the field, the high authorities in Washington themselves failed in the performance of their responsibilities, as the evidence in the conclusions of this report clearly shows.

Nevertheless the commanders in the field were left with sufficient responsibility which they were under obligation to discharge as field commanders of the major outpost in the Pacific defense of the United States. There is adequate and sufficient evidence to show that they failed to discharge that responsibility.

While great emphasis and analysis has been made of such warning messages sent to Admiral Kimmel as those of November 24, 1941, November 27, 1941, and November 28, 1941, attention should be directed to many other messages reflecting the nature of the diplomatic and naval relations between Japan and the United States immediately prior to the attack on Pearl Harbor.

Among these is the message of December 3, 1941, sent from the Washington Office of Naval Operations for action to Admiral Kimmel. This message informed him that Japanese diplomatic posts at Hong Kong, Singapore, Batavia, Manila, Washington, and London had been instructed "to destroy most of their codes and ciphers at once and to burn confidential and secret documents." A second message on the same day sent from Washington to the Commander in Chief of the Asiatic Fleet and marked as information to Admiral Kimmel gave further data on destruction of code machines and secret documents at various places including "all but one copy of other systems" at Washington.

On December 4, 1941, Admiral Kimmel, among others, was informed by Washington Naval Operations that Guam was to destroy all secret and confidential publications, retaining only minimum secret code channels for essential communications and was to be ready instantly to destroy all classified matter retained.

While none of these messages placed Hawaii at the prime center of danger, they certainly reflected the last critical stages in diplomatic relations. It is well known in diplomatic and military circles that destruction of codes, code machines, and secret documents is usually the last step before breaking off relations between governments. War does not necessarily have to follow, but it may follow either simultaneously or close on the heels of the destruction of codes. Other messages and events, supplemented by daily reports of the crisis in Honolulu newspapers, should have raised the significance of the information in the hands of Admiral Kimmel. Yet he testified that he "didn't consider that of any vital importance."

General Short did not receive copies of these messages sent from Washington Naval Operations to Admiral Kimmel regarding the destruction of codes. Admiral Kimmel had the express responsibility, as part of his duty to effect liaison with General Short, to communicate this vital information to General Short. He failed to do so.

Admiral Kimmel should have been aware of the meaning of code destruction and of the Japanese reputation for surprise action. He should have been vigilant. He owed this to his position as commander of the fleet which was closely related to the scene of expected hostilities. Admiral Kimmel failed in the performance of this obligation.

While General Short did not receive the information from Admiral Kimmel that the Japanese were destroying codes and secret papers, he did have partial notice about these developments. At a staff conference on the morning of December 6, in the presence of the Chief of Staff for General Short, Colonel George W. Bicknell had reported that Japanese consuls were burning their papers. General Fielder testified that he was present at the staff conference and informed General Short that the Japanese consul at Honolulu had destroyed his codes and papers.

Before the Roberts Commission General Short testified that he did not know that these consular records were being burned. Later, before our Joint Committee, he corrected this earlier testimony to say that he had been advised on the morning of December 6 that the Honolulu consul was burning his papers. The evidence on this point is not decisive and it is certainly an open question, not determined by the testimony, whether he also knew that the codes were being destroyed.

The evidence as to General Short's knowledge of the burning of papers and the destruction of codes is therefore much less clear and precise than in the ease of Admiral Kimmel. As a contributing factor in the circumstances bearing upon General Short's failure to be prepared to meet the Japanese attack, this evidence must be discounted.

The contribution of the Hawaiian commanders to the Pearl Harbor disaster was the failure of the Army and Navy in Hawaii to institute measures designed to detect an approaching enemy force, to effect state of readiness commensurate with the realization that war was at hand, and to employ every facility at their command in preparing for the Japanese attack, even though these facilities were inadequate. The attack came as an astounding, bewildering, and catastrophic surprise to the commanders at Hawaii. They realized that air attack on Pearl Harbor by Japan was at least a possibility. Specifically, they failed:

(a) To appreciate fully the character of their responsibilities as commanding general of the Hawaiian Department and Commander in Chief of the Pacific Fleet, even though such warnings as they had received from Washington had been inadequate. They failed to carry out the principle of command by mutual cooperation.

(b) To integrate and coordinate their facilities for defense and tighten up their defenses.

(c) To effect liaison on a basis designed to acquaint each with the operations of the other, which was necessary to their joint security and to exchange fully all significant intelligence.

(d) To institute reconnaissance with such limited forces at their disposal on a basis expected to detect an attack from without.

(e) Their radar was in an experimental stage and vital information revealed by it was improperly evaluated; their planes were grouped wing to wing on the field; a large number of officers and men were not at their posts; their ammunition was not immediately at hand for action.

(f) To effect a state of readiness throughout their commands consonant with the character of the warnings sent them and designed to meet an attack from without.

(g) To employ the facilities, materiel, and personnel at their command, which, although limited, were adequate at least to minimize the force of the attack, in repelling the Japanese raiders.

(h) To appreciate the significance of intelligence available at Hawaii affecting the performance of their duties as outpost commanders.

(i) The significance of Japanese submarines sighted early on the morning of December 6 was not properly weighed, and information about such submarines was not diligently transmitted to responsible authorities for action.

The commanding officers in Hawaii had a particular responsibility for the defense of the Pacific Fleet and the Hawaiian coastal frontier. This responsibility they failed to discharge. The failure of the Washington authorities to perform their responsibilities provides extenuating circumstances for the failures of these commanders in the field. These failures in Washington were:

(a) High Washington authorities did not communicate to Admiral Kimmel and General Short adequate information of diplomatic negotiations and of intercepted diplomatic intelligence which, if communicated to them, would have informed them of the imminent menace of a Japanese attack in time for them to fully alert and prepare the defense of Pearl Harbor.

(b) High Washington authorities did not communicate to Admiral Kimmel and General Short such vital intercepted Japanese intelligence information as the "bomb plot" messages and the "dead-line messages" which, if so communicated, would have served as specific warnings of impending hostile attack. In particular, the "bomb plot" messages directly concerned the safety of the fleet and security of the naval base at Pearl Harbor (and at no other place) and if communicated to the Hawaiian commanders would have informed them of specific Japanese designs affecting Pearl Harbor in time for them to alert and prepare their defense.

(c) By conflicting and imprecise messages and orders high Washington authorities created such a condition of confusion relative to what the Hawaiian commanders were to do and were not to do about alerting and preparing for defense at Pearl Harbor, as to remove from such commanders that clear responsibility which would have otherwise attached to them by reason of their positions.

(d) High Washington authorities positively misled the commanders at Hawaii by indicating in messages sent to Hawaii the probability that Japanese hostile actions were likely to take place at points in the Southwestern Pacific without mentioning the danger of attack at Hawaii. From their superior information of Japanese designs and intentions the high Washington authorities were in a better position to evaluate Japanese actions than were the Hawaiian commanders. Having directed the attention of the Hawaiian commanders to probable Japanese action at points other than Pearl Harbor, the high Washington authorities misled the Hawaiian commanders and so contributed to their unpreparedness in the defense of Pearl Harbor.

(e) High Washington authorities took over so much of the detailed direction of affairs respecting operations of the Pacific Fleet and of the Hawaiian naval base as to limit narrowly the discretion and freedom allowed to the Hawaiian commanders. Having thus weakened the individual obligations of the Hawaiian commanders and having failed correspondingly to provide them with clear and adequate orders, high

Washington authorities reduced the responsibility of the Hawaiian commanders in the defense of Pearl Harbor.

(f) Having failed to provide the Hawaiian commanders with sufficient, adequate, and appropriate materiel and equipment for the defense of Hawaii, high Washington authorities compelled the Hawaiian commanders to make choices of action jeopardizing their defense which they would not have made on their own responsibility had they had the needed materiel and equipment; and this failure in Washington was a strong factor in the failure of the defense at Hawaii.

(g) The responsibility of the Hawaiian commanders was further reduced by explicit orders from Washington not to do anything to alarm the civil population and that the high authorities in Washington desired Japan to commit the first overt act.

(h) Having assumed so much of the detailed direction of affairs relating to Hawaiian defense, Washington authorities had the obligation to correct all wrongful decisions at Hawaii which had been made in response to Washington orders. A crucial decision of this kind was made by General Short when he alerted his command only against sabotage in response to orders in the message of November 27, 1941. With superior knowledge of impending danger and having the immediate obligation to correct General Short's error of judgment, Washington authorities, particularly General George C. Marshall and General Leonard T. Gerow, did not do so but permitted General Short to assume that he had done all that had been required of him. This error, as later proved, left the defenses at Hawaii particularly vulnerable to external attack.

(i)   In the critical hours from the afternoon of
      December 6 to 10:30 a.m. on December 7,
      Washington authorities failed to take the instant
      action called for by their special knowledge of
      Japanese messages on those days which would have
      placed the Hawaiian commanders on the specific
      alert for probable danger to Hawaii.

The conclusion that "everybody" in the chain of authority "from the higher officials here in Washington down
through the lieutenant who disregarded the radar message
at Pearl Harbor on Sunday morning, December 7, just
muffed the situation, let the Japs outsmart them," was
expressed by Representative Clark in the form of a question put to Admiral Kimmel. Admiral Kimmel replied: "I
think you should draw those conclusions, sir, rather than
me." Mr Clark then said: "That is all I have, Mr Chairman."

The word "muffed" is colloquial and rhetorical, not
precisely descriptive; and the word "situation" is as vague
as it is general. But Representative Clark's idea translated
into plain English fairly describes events and actions from
November 25 to December 7. "Everybody from the
higher officials here in Washington down through the lieutenant" at Pearl Harbor failed to take many actions that in
the very nature of things were to be expected of him,
failed to discharge obligations necessarily attached to his
office, and must bear a share of the responsibility for the
catastrophe according to the extent of his powers and
duties.

∞≪◊≫∞

In extenuation of failures on the part of high authorities in
Washington two statements were often made by witnesses
who appeared before the Committee. First, it is easy to see

now the mistakes and failures made by high authorities but this is merely "hindsight." Second, those high authorities were busy men carrying heavy burdens in their respective offices—burdens so heavy that many failures on their part must be excused.

Undoubtedly, hindsight is often easier and better than foresight. But the exercise of prudence and foresight with reference to knowledge in his possession is a bounden duty imposed on every high authority in the Government of the United States by the powers and obligations of his office. For every failure to exercise prudence and foresight with reference to knowledge in his possession he must bear a corresponding burden of responsibility for the consequences that flow from that failure. By virtue of his office he is presumed to have special competence and knowledge; to act upon his special knowledge, and to be informed and alert in the discharge of his duties in the situation before him.

The introduction of hindsight in extenuation of responsibility is, therefore, irrelevant to the determination of responsibility for the catastrophe at Pearl Harbor.

The question before this Committee is: What did high authorities in Washington know about Japanese designs and intentions; what decisions did they make on the basis of their knowledge; and what actions did they take to safeguard the security of the American outposts?

With regard to General Marshall and Admiral Stark, they were certainly carrying heavy burdens in preparing the armed forces of the United States for war; in making war plans; in building up an Army and Navy (which they knew were not yet ready for war); and in struggling for a postponement of the war until the Army and Navy were better prepared to cope with the foe. With regard to the President, the Secretary of State, the Secretary of War, and the Secretary of the Navy, it may be said justly that they were carrying heavy burdens also. But all these officials, as Secretary Stimson's diary demonstrates, spent many days before December 7 in general discussions which led to no decisions. This they did at a time when they possessed special knowledge of Japanese designs and were acquainted with their own intentions and resolves and certainly had the leisure to do the one obvious duty dictated by common sense—that is—draw up a brief plan for telling the outpost commanders just what to do in a certain contingency on receipt of orders from Washington.

That contingency was a Japanese attack on American possessions somewhere. Secretary Stimson records that "the question (during those days) was how we (the President, Secretary Hull, Secretary Stimson, Secretary Knox, General Marshall, and Admiral Stark) should maneuver them (the Japanese) into the position of firing the first shot without allowing too much damage to ourselves." In any event, inasmuch as the President decided against appealing to Congress for a declaration of war on Japan, they were all waiting for the Japanese to fire the first shot! And in those circumstances it was their duty to prepare definite plans and procedures for action in meeting that attack.

This is exactly what they did not do at any time before December 7. They had plans for action or actions by the armed forces of the United States if Congress declared war or if by some process the United States got into or entered the war. War plans (for example, Rainbow No. 5 which was WPL-6) were to go into operation only after war had begun and were not intended for preparation in meeting surprise attack.

They prepared no plan giving the outpost commanders instructions about the measures they were to take in preparing for and meeting a Japanese attack on American possessions when and if it came. This plan could have been drawn up in a few hours at most and set down in two or three typewritten pages at most. With modifications appropriate to the various outposts this plan could have been sent to the respective commanders by couriers or swifter means of communication.

And a procedure could have been adopted for instructing the commanders by one word in code, or a few words, to put plans for meeting Japanese attack into effect. No such plan was drawn up or at all events no such plan was sent to the commanders. No procedure for giving them the code word or words for action under any plan or procedure was ever adopted by the authorities in Washington whose official duty it was to prepare, with all the resources at their command, for meeting the Japanese attack, which they privately recognized as an imminent menace.

∞⚬❦⚬∞

Of particular infractions of duty in Washington, which were numerous and are written large in the evidence before the Committee, a few illustrations may be given in summary form.

Secretary Stimson and Secretary Hull were in a substantial measure responsible for the confusion that resulted in equivocal form of the so-called warning message to General Short on November 27.

Secretary Stimson called up Secretary Hull early in the morning of November 27 and Secretary Hull declared positively: "I have washed my hands of it and it is now in the hands of you and Knox—the Army and the Navy."

Secretary Stimson then called up President Roosevelt and the President gave him "a little different view." But from the President, that day, Secretary Stimson got the President's approval—"that we should send the final alert namely that he [General Short along with other commanders] should be on the qui vive for any attack."

Secretary Stimson and General Gerow started the draft of the warning message with the words: "Negotiations with Japan have been terminated." Secretary Stimson, after a conversation with Secretary Hull over the telephone, altered this definite statement to read: "Negotiations with Japan appear to be terminated to all practical purposes with only the barest possibilities that the Japanese Government might come back to continue," thus introducing confusion into a sentence of crucial importance.

General Marshall and General Gerow admitted to the Committee that they made a mistake in failing to reply to General Short's report to the War Department on November 27, that he put into effect the alert against sabotage. This reply referred to the message of November 27 by number so there could be no mistake as to what it answered. It was in reply to the words of the message to Short on November 27 and the words "report measures taken." They also assumed full responsibility for that mistake.

General Marshall could not recall that he had made, after November 27, any inquiries as to the measures taken by General Short in Hawaii. In other words, he apparently had no information about the steps taken for the defense of Pearl Harbor during the 10 critical days of mounting war tension, when Washington authorities were, through intercepts of Japanese messages, becoming increasingly certain about Japan's steps toward war, except General Short was alerted to sabotage and had liaison with the Navy. Alerted to sabotage meant the planes were bunched on the field and in no position to take to the air quickly.

Responsible officers in the War Department told the Committee they failed to reach General Marshall after the receipt of the first 13 parts of the Japanese memorandum had been intercepted late in the afternoon of December 6. General Marshall testified that he had an orderly at his home to receive calls when he was away at night and hence he could have been reached. He also testified that he was unaware of any effort to locate him at his home or elsewhere by messenger or telephone during the evening of December 6—or the morning of December 7—until he was taking his shower after a ride in the park.

Secretary Stimson interfered with efforts of General Marshall and General Gerow to postpone the breach with Japan until the Army and Navy were ready to meet a Japanese attack with better prospects of success. The Secretary insisted that in asking for the delay no recommendation should be made to the President advising a reopening of conversations with the Japanese representatives. In fact, conversations had not been formally closed on November 26.

Secretary Hull made "several general statements" to General Marshall on diplomatic matters but did not read to him or give him a copy of the November 26 memorandum to Japan in advance of delivery. Secretary Hull gave confused and conflicting statements to Secretary Stimson, Secretary Knox, General Marshall, and Admiral Stark and, so far as the evidence before the Committee goes, Secretary Hull did not at any time tell them definitely that relations with Japan were ipso facto ruptured, as he had learned from intercepted Japanese messages. In other words, Secretary Hull's words and actions during the last few weeks of tension added to the uncertainty that reigned in the War and Navy Departments. Despite all his conferences with representatives of the two Departments, he went ahead changing his plans and notions without giving them information respecting his crucial decisions.

It was with sufficient reason that Admiral Stark, on November 25, wrote a letter to Admiral Kimmel, saying:

> I won't go into the pros and cons of what the United
> States may do. I will be damned if I know. I wish I did.
> The only thing I do know is that we may do most
> anything, and that's the only thing I know to be prepared
> for; or we may do nothing—I think it is more likely to be
> "anything,"

This letter reached Admiral Kimmel on December 3, adding to the confusion already created by the war-warning message of November 27.

This message to Admiral Kimmel differed in one respect from the message sent by the War Department to General Short: it stated definitely that "the negotiations with Japan have ended." But not content with that, the Navy Department, two days later, sent to Admiral Kimmel another dispatch quoting the War Department's message to General Short as follows: "Negotiations with Japan appear to be terminated with only the barest possibility of resumption."

After stating in its message of November 27 that "Japan is expected to make an aggressive move within the next few days," the Navy Department immediately added: "An amphibious expedition against either the Philippines, Thai, or Kra Peninsula or possibly Borneo is possibly indicated." Since there was not a line in the message about a possible expedition against Hawaii, these words, according to legal and common-sense usage, warranted Admiral Kimmel in concluding that an attack on Pearl Harbor was not expected by the Navy Department and that he was not to expect such an attack.

In explaining to Representative Keefe how he expected Admiral Kimmel to expect an attack on Pearl Harbor in view of the fact that the Navy Department's message mentioned only points in the Far East as possible points of attack, Admiral Stark gave probably the best explanation available to him:

> That is true, but the attack we envisaged down there we stated that the makeup and so forth of this amphibious expedition, not a raiding force or a carrier force, but an amphibious expedition and the points of that amphibious expedition might be so and so. There was no question, there had not been in my mind at any time, of an amphibious expedition against the Hawaiian Island.

Of the many instances showing failures of Washington authorities to cooperate and keep one another duly informed when such acts of duty were vital to the interests of the United States, none was more fateful than actions on the so-called modus vivendi proposed by Japan on November 20, 1941.

Item 1 of the Japanese proposal read: "Both the Governments of Japan and the United States undertake not to make any armed advancement into any of the regions in the Southeastern and Southern Pacific area excepting the part of French Indo-China where Japanese troops are stationed."

Item 2 read: "The Japanese Government undertakes to withdraw its troops now stationed in French Indo-China upon either the restoration of peace between Japan and China or the establishment of an equitable peace in the Pacific area."

Wholly apart from the merits or demerits of these and other items in the Japanese proposal of November 20, here was an opportunity at least to prolong "the breathing spell" for which General Marshall and Admiral Stark were pleading in their efforts to strengthen the armed forces of the United States for war. On November 5, General Marshall and Admiral Stark presented a strong plea to the President begging for time in which to make the Army and Navy ready for war. While the Japanese proposal for a modus vivendi was under consideration by the President and Secretary Hull, General Marshall and Admiral Stark prepared another plea for the postponement of the breach with Japan so that the Army and Navy could be made stronger in striking or defensive power. They did not ask for any surrender of American principles; they merely called for delay.

The Japanese proposal for a modus vivendi offered an opportunity to stop for a few weeks the advance of Japanese armed forces into the Southeastern and Southern area—the advance which, according to American war plans, made in cooperation with British and Dutch officers, provided for American action against Japan or American participation in a war against Japan. It is true that President Roosevelt had not committed the United States officially to these plans but, according to the testimony of Admiral Stark, "the President except officially, approved of" the basic principles of these plans. American official War Plan WPL-46 was based on them. Whether written in binding agreements or not, American, British, and Dutch authorities acted in concert just as if binding pacts had been made. The Japanese, as Washington clearly learned from the intercepts, also acted upon the assumption that American, British, and Dutch agreements for concerted action existed.

President Roosevelt evidently deemed it both feasible and desirable to reach some kind of modus vivendi with Japan with a view to a possible settlement in general, or in any event a prolongation of negotiations with Japan until

American armed forces were better prepared for war. Proof of this was found in a penciled memorandum written by the President for the Secretary of State "not dated but probably written shortly after November 20, 1941," that is, after the receipt of the Japanese proposal.

President Roosevelt's memorandum for Secretary Hull with regard to the possible terms of the modus vivendi with Japan read:

6 MONTHS
1. US to resume economic relations—some oil and rice now—more later.
2. Japan to send no more troops to Indo-China or Manchurian border or any place South (Dutch, Brit. or Siam).
3. Japan not to invoke tripartite pact even if the US gets into European war.
4. US to introduce Japs to Chinese to talk things over but US to take no part in their conversation.
★ ★ ★
Later in Pacific agreements.

Besides the President's instructions or suggestions, Secretary Hull had before him the "outline of a proposed basis for agreement between the United States and Japan," which had been carefully prepared by Henry Morgenthau, Jr, Secretary of the Treasury. Henry Morgenthau's "outline" with a covering note, dated November 19, 1941, was presented to Secretary Hull, initialled M. M. H. (Maxwell M. Hamilton, Chief of the Division of Far Eastern Affairs). The covering note informed Secretary Hull that all the senior officers of the Division concurred with Mr Hamilton in the view that "the proposal is the most constructive one I have seen." Mr Hamilton urged Secretary Hull to give most careful consideration to the proposal promptly, and suggested that the Secretary make copies of the proposed "outline" available to Admiral Stark and General Marshall and arrange to confer with them as soon as they had had an opportunity to examine the "outline."

With the President's instructions or suggestions and Secretary Morgenthau's "outline" before him, Secretary Hull considered the terms of a possible agreement with Japan as the basis of a general settlement or an indefinite continuation of negotiations in connection with the Japanese proposal for a modus vivendi. This is no place to give a 50-page summary of the record of the events connected with Secretary Hull's operations. Nor is it necessary to discuss the merits of the case. But the following recital of facts illustrates the confusion and lack of cooperation that prevailed in Administration circles.

Secretary Hull drafted a memorandum for at least a kind of truce with Japan. Secretary Hull discussed his proposals with British, Dutch, and Australian representatives in Washington. Secretary Hull had a conference on the proposals with Secretary Stimson and Secretary Knox at his office on November 25. Of this conference Secretary Stimson noted in his diary:

> Hull showed us the proposal for a three months' truce, which he was going to lay before the Japanese today or tomorrow. It adequately safeguarded all our interests, I thought as I read it, but I don't think there is any chance of the Japanese accepting it, because it was so drastic.

The next day, November 26, Secretary Hull told Secretary Stimson over the telephone that he had about made up his mind not to give the proposal for the three months' truce to the Japanese but "to kick the whole thing over." Under pressure coming from Chiang Kai-shek, Winston Churchill and others, relative to the modus vivendi, Secretary Hull refrained from making an independent decision on this important step and it appears he was led to decide it without thought of the military capacities necessary to back up our diplomatic position. On that day, November 26, Secretary Hull, with the approval of President Roosevelt, kicked the whole thing over and sent to the Japanese the now famous memorandum which Japan treated as an ultimatum. In taking this action Secretary Hull gave no advance notice to General Marshall and Admiral Stark, who were then preparing their second careful memorandum to the President begging for a postponement of war with Japan until the Army and Navy could make better preparation for waging it. Moreover, it should be noted that Secretary Hull did not give to the British and Australian representatives any advance information about his sudden decision "to kick the whole thing over."

When Secretary Hull, with the approval of President Roosevelt, made this decision on November 26 and handed his memorandum to the Japanese ambassadors on November 26, he was practically certain that the Japanese Government would reject his proposals and that a break in relations would be a highly probable consequence of his action.

For this statement there is sufficient evidence from Secretary Hull himself. In his account of the meeting with the Japanese representatives, when he presented the memorandum to them, Secretary Hull reported that, after reading the document, Mr Kurusu said "that when this proposal of the United States was reported to the Japanese Government, that Government would be likely to 'throw up its hands'; that this response to the Japanese proposal (the so-called modus vivendi proposal from Tokyo) could be interpreted as tantamount to the end of the negotiations." So certain was Secretary Hull of the coming breach that, according to his account, he declared on November 25 and November 28 at a meeting of "high officials" that "the matter of safeguarding our national security was in the hands of the Army and Navy." Some exchanges with the Japanese occurred after November 27, 1941, but none of these exchanges altered in any respect the situation created by Secretary Hull's memorandum of November 26 to Japan.

If Secretary Hull or any other high authority in Washington had any doubt whether the Japanese would treat the memorandum of November 26 to Japan as an ultimatum, that doubt must have been entirely cleared up two days later. On November 28, the Army intercepted a message from Tokyo to the two Japanese ambassadors in Washington which expressed the views of the Japanese Government on Secretary Hull's document. The Japanese message characterized it as "this humiliating proposal" and as "quite unexpected and extremely regrettable." The Japanese message also informed the ambassadors that the reply of the Japanese Government would come in two or three days and that "the negotiations will be de facto ruptured. This is inevitable." Washington also knew that the dead-line had been fixed for November 29, and that after that "things would automatically happen." The Japanese ambassadors were instructed not to give the impression that "the negotiations are broken off" and told: "From now on do the best you can."

In short, on November 28, 1941, Washington authorities had available to them definite and conclusive information that the breach with Japan was near at hand and that the reply from Tokyo would signalize that breach. More definitely than the first 13 parts of the Japanese message intercepted on the evening of December 6, this notice from Tokyo to its representatives in Washington on November 28 meant a rupture of relations with the United States. If the 13 parts meant war to the President, the Japanese message on November 28 also meant war. Hawaii knew nothing of these intercepts of December 6 and 7 until after the attack.

These instances of failure on the part of high authorities in Washington to perform acts of duty and judgment required by their respective offices, and many others that could be cited, merely point to the greatest failure of all, namely, the failure of those authorities to organize for the war they regarded as immediately imminent. Here the conclusions reached by the Army Pearl Harbor Board as to the War Department apply to the whole executive department of which it was a part:

> A few men, without organization in a true sense, were
> attempting to conduct large enterprises, take multiple
> actions, and give directions that should have been the result
> of carefully directed commands, instead of actions taken by
> conference. We were preparing for war by the conference
> method. We were directing such preparations by the
> conference method; we were even writing vital messages
> by the conference method, and arriving at their content by
> compromise instead of by command.

To this comment, the Army Pearl Harbor Board should have added that powerful individuals among these authorities were reaching decisions on their own motion and taking actions of a dangerous nature on their own motion, despite all the conferring, talking, and compromising, were proceeding as if there was no organization in the Government of the United States that was charged with preparing for and waging war.

Nor is this confusion and pulling at cross purposes to be explained away by any such vague assertion as the Army Pearl Harbor Board offered: "that it was a product of the time and conditions due to the transition from peace to war in a democracy." Failures to perform duties commensurate with the powers vested in officials by the Constitution and the law cannot be justified by appeals to any overriding requirements of democracy. Provisions for organizing the Executive Department and the supreme command of the armed forces of the United States were incorporated in the Constitution and the laws, and adequate powers to organize and unify for operating purposes all subsidiary agencies were vested in the President of the United States.

Going down the line along the chain of authority to the commanders in Hawaii, it must be said that General Short and Admiral Kimmel were as negligent in certain respects as their superiors in Washington. They were aware that a Japanese attack at some point was impending and, despite any general expectation that the attack would come in the Far East, they were under obligations to be intently on guard themselves. But they failed to affect the close cooperation, especially between December 3 and December 7, that was required by their special knowledge and official duties. Each of them showed an unwarranted indifference to what the other was doing in the way of scanning the horizon, watching for signs of trouble, and preparing for the worst. Finally, they failed to make the best and most efficient disposition and use of the material they possessed in the discharge of grave responsibilities imposed on them.

Failure of the President to take action on December 6 and 7

In the final instance of crucial significance for alerting the American outpost commanders, on Saturday night, December 6 and Sunday morning, December 7, the President of the United States failed to take that quick and instant executive action which was required by the occasion and by the responsibility for watchfulness and guardianship rightly associated in law and practice with his high office from the establishment of the Republic to our own times.

Before noon on Saturday of December 6, 1941, the President was aware that a situation had been established which, by a unanimous decision of himself and his War Cabinet reached eight days before, made an American–Japanese war a matter of a very few hours. He and his Secretaries of State, War, and Navy, and his Chief of Staff and Chief of Naval Operations, had discussed on November 28 the presence of a Japanese expeditionary force at sea. It was their decision that if this expeditionary force got around the southern point of Indo-China, it would be a terrific blow to the British, Dutch, and Americans. "This must not be allowed." It was agreed that if the Japanese got into the Isthmus of Kra, the British would fight and if the British fought we would have to fight. "And it now seems clear that if this expedition were allowed to round the southern point of Indo-China, this whole chain of disastrous events would be set on foot." At 10:40 on the morning of December 6, the State Department was advised by Ambassador Winant that the British had sighted a Japanese task force in the South China Sea and Gulf of Siam headed for the Kra Peninsula or Thailand. The Japanese had passed the southern point of Indo-China.

In testifying before the Joint Committee as to the significance of this information Under Secretary Welles said: "I should say that the chances had diminished from one in a thousand to one in a million that war could then be avoided." No word of this situation went to the American commanders at Pearl Harbor.

Although the War Cabinet, as early as November 28, had anticipated the situation of noon of December 6 as making war inevitable, the Chief of Staff and the Chief of Naval Operations not only did not advise the commanders in the field as to this situation, but also exhibited so little concern approximately 20 hours later that the Chief of Staff went horseback riding on the morning of December 7 and the Chief of Naval Operations, having spent the evening at a theater, got to his office late on the morning of the 7th. Each of these officers knew on the morning of December 7 that a Pacific war would start within a few hours and, by their own judgment and that of the President, that such war must involve the United States. In the light of the situation known to them and to the President and his Secretaries of State, War, and Navy on the morning of December 7, and in view of the decisions reached in anticipation of such a situation, an alert should have been sent to Hawaii prior to the alert sent by commercial facilities by General Marshall on December 7 at 11:50 a.m., which alert did not reach the Hawaiian commanders prior to the attack—the November 27 and all prior alerts having been confusing, misleading, and imprecise.

Before 10 o'clock on the evening of December 6, 1941, President Roosevelt had reached a great decision as to the immediate imminence of the war which he had long expected. He had then finished reading the first 13 parts of the intercepted memorandum which was to be presented to Secretary Hull by the Japanese ambassador and special agent on the next day, and had said to his aide, Harry Hopkins, in substance, "This means war." In reply to a comment by Mr Hopkins, the President had also indicated that the United States could not strike the first blow for the purpose of preventing any sort of surprise.

The President's evaluation of the intelligence before him as to the probable day, hour, and place of the coming Japanese attack is nowhere in the evidence before this Committee. But, given all the information that had come to him during the preceding days, he had every reason for assuming that the day and hour could not be far off. The place on which the first Japanese blow would fall was within the territory and possessions of the United State where outpost commanders were on guard.

Between 10 o'clock on the evening of December 6 and the Japanese attack on Pearl Harbor 16 hours were to pass. The President had at his disposal at least 15 hours in which to inform those outpost commanders of impending danger, to add new and urgent warning to the indefinite warnings that had been sent out during previous days and weeks.

The President's acquaintance with the nature of warfare, and it was by no means elementary, must have convinced him that the consequences of the first magnitude would flow from the success or failure of the United States armed forces in meeting the Japanese attack when it came. Unqualified success on the part of the American forces could wreck Japanese war plans and cripple Japanese armed forces. Disaster to the armed forces of the United States could, and probably would, prolong the war for months or years.

In this situation, having decided about 10 p.m. December 6, that the intercepted message meant war, the most imperative duty that confronted the President was that of alerting his immediate subordinates in Washington and, either directly or through them, the outpost commanders. This duty was imposed upon him by the circumstances and by the obligations of his office as Chief Executive and Commander in Chief of the armed forces of the United States—in peace and war. Of all the men in the branches of civil and military administration responsible for the security and defense of the United States, the President alone was endowed with ultimate power under the Constitution and the laws. Means of swift communication were at his elbow. Willing aides—civil and military and naval—were at his beck and call.

The most powerful men next to the President in authority—men bound to obey his orders and serve without stint, were not far from the President's side; and anyone of them, if so instructed, could have found and alerted all the others. Secretary Hull, Secretary Stimson, Secretary Knox, General Marshall, and Admiral Stark were nearby. They could be reached quickly by means of communication at the President's command.

Indeed, Captain Alwin D. Kramer, who had carried the 13-part intercept to the White House for delivery to President Roosevelt by Commander Schulz, immediately turned his attention to the task of alerting the President's chief subordinates. Captain Kramer tried to reach Admiral Stark by telephone and failed; he likewise failed to reach Admiral Turner.

Thereupon Captain Kramer telephoned to Secretary Knox, found him at home, and took to Secretary Knox the intercepted message and other documents. After the receipt of the papers, Secretary Knox, realizing at once their significant nature, called up Secretary Hull and Secretary Stimson and arranged with them for a meeting at the State Department on Sunday morning at 10 o'clock. Having completed this arrangement Secretary Knox instructed Captain Kramer to bring all the important messages in question to the State Department at 10 o'clock Sunday morning Thus, as Captain Kramer testified, on Saturday night he had reached the top man in the White House and the top man in the Navy.

According to the testimony of Colonel Rufus Bratton, chief of the Far Eastern Section, Military Intelligence Division, of the War Department, the 13–part message was sent to the State Department on Saturday night. Colonel Bratton stated:

> So I, realizing that the Secretary of State was primarily interested in this message, it being a diplomatic one and it being a reply to a message that he had sent to the Japanese Government, gathered up his folder, put it in the pouch, locked the pouch, and personally delivered it to the night duty officer in the State Department sometime after 10 o'clock that night. I told the night duty officer whose name I have forgotten, that this was a highly important message as far as the Secretary of State was concerned, and that I would like to have it sent out to his quarters. He assured me that he would do so. I left it with him, securing from him a receipt for what I had given him.

Thus it is evident that about 10 o'clock Saturday night President Roosevelt could have reached Secretary Hull, Secretary Stimson, and Secretary Knox in a few minutes, had he chosen to do so.

What about General Marshall and Admiral Stark, to whom the President under the law could go directly with orders for operations? If not at home, they should have been in places known to their orderlies or assistants, for the War and Navy Departments had been alerted, lights were burning all night in offices of those Departments; and responsible officers were there waiting for news and orders. News of the intercepted Japanese messages had been delivered to Army authorities about nine o'clock that night—before it had been delivered to Secretary Knox, head of the Navy Department.

The White House was alerted. The President's naval aid was standing by at the White House on the evening of December 6. Within less than an hour President Roosevelt, convinced that the 13-part message meant war, could have brought to his side one or more of the four men immediately responsible for war action under his direction, could have taken council with them, and could decide upon the orders necessary to alert all the outpost commanders before midnight.

In this situation with these powers and obligations entrusted to him, what did the President do? Recognizing the gravity of the hour and the occasion, he was moved to act—at first. He tried to reach by telephone the Chief of Naval Operations, Admiral Stark, and at the first attempt failed. Apparently it was reported to the President that Admiral Stark was at a theater. What then? According to the testimony of Commander Schulz, who had brought the 13-part message to the President's room in the White House, the President said in the presence of the commander, that he did not want to cause any undue alarm by having Admiral Stark paged or otherwise notified in the theater, "because he [the President] could get him [Admiral Stark] within perhaps another half hour."

Apparently the President did communicate with Admiral Stark later that evening. But the evidence before the Committee is indirect, for Admiral Stark's mind seems to be a complete blank as to his whereabouts and doings on the evening of December 6, 1941. When he testified before the Committee at its regular hearings, the admiral was under the firm impression that he did not talk with the President over the telephone on that evening, but then confessed that he might be mistaken. Later however, at a special session of the Committee on May 31, 1946, Admiral Stark testified that a friend, Captain H. D. Krick, had recently given him some information on the point. Captain Krick had informed Admiral Stark that they had been together on the evening of December 6, 1941 and that the admiral had been in communication with the President over the telephone. But this recent information did not refresh the admiral's memory, for he declared at the special session of the Committee that he still had "no recollection whatever of any events of that evening." With regard to anything that passed between the President and Admiral Stark that evening, assuming that Captain Krick's memory is good, the record before this Committee is as empty as Admiral Stark's mind.

What did the President do on Sunday morning between his rising hour and about 1:25 p.m. (Eastern standard time, 7:55 Honolulu time) when the Japanese attack on Pearl Harbor began?

During this lapse of hours, additional news of Japanese designs was in Washington. About 5 o'clock in the morning of December 7, the fourteenth part of the Japanese message reached the Navy Department. Although it could have been decoded in less than half an hour, that operation was delayed in the office and this fourteenth part did not come into the hands of Captain Kramer until about 7:30 a.m. Another inexplicable delay occurred. Captain Kramer did not deliver this message to the White House until 10 or 15 minutes before 10 on Sunday morning. But two hours or more then remained in which to put the outpost commanders on full defensive war alert.

On or about 10:30 on Sunday morning, two other highly informative messages were delivered at the White House.

The first was the intercepted Japanese Government message instructing the Japanese ambassador to deliver the

14-part reply to the Secretary of State at 1 p.m. December 7 (Washington time). The second was a message from Tokyo to the Japanese embassy in Washington, marked "extremely urgent." It ordered Japanese agents, after deciphering the fourteenth part to destroy at once the remaining cipher machines and all machine codes—a notice that carried a war warning to high authorities in Washington.

Meanwhile General Marshall, who testified that he did not see President Roosevelt between November 28 and the afternoon of December 7, reached his post in the War Department. Before him lay the final 14-part message and the message stating that the delivery to Secretary Hull was to be at 1 o'clock. On the basis of this and other information, in his possession, General Marshall concluded that war was at hand, that the hour "one o'clock" was indicative of "some very definite action" by the Japanese at 1 o'clock, and that a new and definite warning message should go to General Short—the message that did not reach General Short until the Japanese attack on Pearl Harbor was over.

During the hours from 10 o'clock Saturday night to 11 o'clock Sunday morning, President Roosevelt had at his command not only the latest intercepts and his own knowledge of diplomatic negotiations with Great Britain and Japan, but also special knowledge that had come to him before the evening of December 6; for example: The message from Tokyo to the Japanese ambassador in Berlin telling him to see Hitler and Ribbentrop and "say very secretly to them that there is extreme danger that war may suddenly break out between the Anglo-Saxon nations and Japan," and the message transmitted at 10:40 o'clock in the morning of December 6 by Ambassador Winant in London from the British Admiralty, stating that large Japanese expeditionary forces were moving swiftly toward Kra, a threat which was to bring into play American–British war plans for combined action against Japan unless the President refused to give official sanction to the plans he had approved "except officially."

Knowing all these things and more besides, including the zero hour of 1 o'clock fixed by the Japanese Government for the delivery of the message that meant a de facto rupture of relations, unable under the Constitution to commit the overt act of striking Japan at once, waiting for the Japanese to fire "the first shot without allowing too much danger to ourselves," President Roosevelt was under direct and immediate obligation to make certain that urgent messages be sent to the outpost commanders, including General Short and Admiral Kimmel, and sent not later than 11 o'clock on Sunday morning by the swiftest possible means of communication.

For his failure to take this action Saturday night, December 6, or early Sunday morning, December 7, President Roosevelt must bear a responsibility commensurate with his powers and duties under the Constitution, with his position as Commander in Chief of the Army and Navy, and with the trust vested in him as the Chief Executive by the people of the United States.

American people not to blame for Pearl Harbor

The contention committing from so high an authority as President Truman on August 3, 1945, that the "country is as much to blame as any individual in this final situation that developed in Pearl Harbor," cannot be sustained because the American people had no intimation whatever of the policies and operations that were being undertaken.

How could the desire of the American people in the months before December 7, 1941, to keep out of war be responsible for the specific failures of Washington and Hawaii in the defense of Pearl Harbor? How could

Congress be to blame for unpreparedness when it enacted into law greater defense appropriations than the President and his Budget Bureau recommended? How could the American people be held responsible for the secret diplomacy of Washington authorities? They were never advised of the many secret undertakings by Washington authorities. Indeed, the high authorities in Washington seemed to be acting upon some long-range plan which was never disclosed to Congress or to the American people.

A nation in mortal danger is entitled to know the truth about its peril. If foreign policy and diplomatic representations are treated as the exclusive secret information of the President and his advisers, public opinion will not be enlightened. A people left in the dark by their leaders cannot be held responsible for the consequences of their leader's actions.

On December 1, 1941, it was known to the Secretary of War and to the President and his close advisers that Japan had informed Hitler on December 1 that war was imminent. They knew this by intercepting the following message from Tokyo to Berlin:

[Secret]
From: Tokyo
To: Berlin
November 30, 1941
#985. (Part 1 of 3)
Re my Circular #2387
1. The conversations begun between Tokyo and
Washington last April during the administration of the
former cabinet, in spite of the sincere efforts of the
Imperial Government, now stand ruptured-broken. In the
face of this, our Empire faces a grave situation and must
act with determination. Will Your Honor therefore,
immediately interview Chancellor HITLER and Foreign

Minister RIBBENTROP and confidentially communicate to them a summary of the developments. Say to them that lately England and the United States have taken a provocative attitude, both of them. Say that they are planning to move military forces into various places in East Asia and that we will inevitably have to counter by also moving troops. Say very secretly to them that there is extreme danger that war may suddenly break out between the Anglo-Saxon nations and Japan through some clash of arms and add that the time of the breaking out of this war may come quicker than anyone dreams.

Translated 12-141 (NR)

Army 25552 JD: 6943

The Secretary of War, the President and his advisers also were fully aware that Japanese military movements were under way and that these movements would involve the United States in war.

Notwithstanding this intimate knowledge of the imminence of war, the Secretary of War told the American people as late as December 5 that the negotiations with Japan were still in progress. Also, despite the extreme gravity of the situation, known fully to the "War Cabinet," the President permitted the Senate and the House of Representatives to adjourn on December 4 and 5 respectively until noon of December 8 without having informed them of the impending danger to the country.

This seems to follow consistently the understanding observed by Mr Hull when he gave to the President a proposed draft of a message to Congress which was never used. Mr Hull said: "I think we agree that you will not send a message to Congress until the last stage of our relations, relating to actual hostilities."

How could the American people be responsible for the warlike operations conducted from Washington over which the people had no control and about which they were never informed?

In the future the people and their Congress must know how close American diplomacy is moving to war so that they may check its advance if imprudent and support its position if sound. A diplomacy which relies upon the enemy's first overt act to insure effective popular support for the Nation's final war decision is both outmoded and dangerous in the atomic age. To prevent any future Pearl Harbor more tragic and damaging than that of December 7, 1941, there must be constant close coordination between American public opinion and American diplomacy. Eternal vigilance is still the price of liberty even in the atomic era.

Whether or not the Pearl Harbor tragedy could have been avoided by diplomatic means is a most appropriate matter for consideration by all concerned with the 3,000 American boys who there lost their lives.

Exhaustive attention has been given to the military aspects of the events leading up to Pearl Harbor and an invaluable record has been compiled for future students of the situation.

A far less complete record has been written of its diplomatic aspects and here there is the most urgent need of further exploration in justice to the future generations of Americans who may learn here a little of the lessons for which America has paid so great a price.

How to avoid war and how to turn war—if it finally comes—to serve the cause of human progress is the challenge to diplomacy today as yesterday. Here, too, much cannot be known regarding all the petty episodes that finally add up to war. No war comes in a moment. War is the sum of many minor decisions and some that are major. In this diplomatic aspect the Pearl Harbor investigation has sadly failed to live up to the lofty prospectus with which it was launched.

In the light of these facts and of the foregoing conclusions, the charge that the "country" is to blame for what happened at Pearl Harbor cannot be sustained.

CONCLUSIONS

In our opinion, the evidence before this Committee indicates that the tragedy at Pearl Harbor was primarily a failure of men and not of laws or powers to do the necessary things, and carry out the vested responsibilities. No legislation could have cured such defects of official judgment, management, cooperation, and action as were displayed by authorities and agents of the United States in connection with the events that culminated in the catastrophe at Pearl Harbor on December 7, 1941.

This demonstrates the weakness of depending on the political head of the Government to bring about the necessary coordination of the activities of the military branches, particularly in the area of intelligence, and unification of command. The major lesson to be learned is that this coordination should be accomplished in advance of a crisis.

Summary of responsibilities

Having examined the whole record made before the Joint Committee and having analyzed the same in the foregoing Conclusions of Fact and Responsibility, we find the evidence supports the following final and ultimate conclusion:

The failure of Pearl Harbor to be fully alerted and prepared for defense rested upon the proper discharge of two sets of interdependent responsibilities: (1) the responsibilities of high authorities in Washington; and (2) the responsibilities of the commanders in the field in charge of the fleet and of the naval base.

The evidence clearly shows that these two areas of responsibilities were inseparably essential to each other in the defense of Hawaii. The commanders in the field could not have prepared or been ready successfully to meet hostile attack at Hawaii without indispensable information, materiel, trained manpower and clear orders from Washington. Washington could not be certain that Hawaii was in readiness without the alert and active cooperation of the commanders on the spot.

The failure to perform the responsibilities indispensably essential to the defense of Pearl Harbor rests upon the following civil and military authorities: Franklin D. Roosevelt (President of the United States and Commander in Chief of the Army and Navy); Henry L. Stimson (Secretary of War); Frank Knox (Secretary of the Navy); George C. Marshall (General, Chief of Staff of the Army); Harold R. Stark (Admiral, Chief of Naval Operations); Leonard T. Gerow (Major General, Assistant Chief of Staff of War Plans Division).

The failure to perform the responsibilities in Hawaii rests upon the military commanders: Walter C. Short (Major General, Commanding General, Hawaiian Department); Husband E. Kimmel (Rear Admiral, Commander in Chief of the Pacific Fleet).

Both in Washington and in Hawaii there were numerous and serious failures of men in the lower civil and military echelons to perform their duties and discharge their responsibilities. These are too numerous to be treated in detail and individually named.

Secretary of State, Cordell Hull, who was at the center of Japanese–American negotiations bears a grave responsibility for the diplomatic conditions leading up to the eventuality of Pearl Harbor but he had no duties as a relevant link in the military chain of responsibility stemming from the Commander in Chief to the commanders at Hawaii for the defense at Pearl Harbor. For this reason and because the diplomatic phase was not completely explored we offer no conclusions in his case.

HOMER FERGUSON
OWEN BREWSTER

Other titles in the series

Escape from Germany, 1939–45

"It is quite certain that, apart from the microphone, no evidence whatever had been found to show a tunnel was being dug, yet in the four-and-a-half months from the commencement of the tunnel campaign, more than 166 tons of sand had been excavated from three tunnels and hidden in a compound only a mile in circumference which was constantly patrolled and inspected by Germans."

Backdrop

The history of Air Force captivity in Germany began on 3 September 1939, the day Britain declared war on Germany. On the same day, a New Zealand officer was shot down over the North Sea and was subsequently taken prisoner. By December 1939, the numbers of those captured had grown, and the Germans began to segregate Air Force prisoners, housing them in special camps.

The Book

Of the 10,000 British airmen held as prisoners-of-war by the Germans during World War II, less than 30 successfully managed to find their way back to Britain or to a neutral country. After 1945, many escapers and PoWs were interviewed, and a file was built up of their various experiences. This file was kept secret for nearly 40 years (despite the fact that several famous films were made about these escapes), as it was thought to contain evidence of enterprise and resilience that could still be useful to an enemy. Now "uncovered" for the public to read, this book contains the true and often incredible stories of the heroic attempts of these men to escape. Drawn from the narratives of the men themselves, it includes such remarkable stories as "The Trojan Horse"—a hollow vaulting horse that was used to disguise a tunnel entrance—and the persistent and ingenious attempts to escape made from camps such as the formidable Colditz.

ISBN 0 11 702459 7   Price £6.99

War in the Falklands, 1982

"On 22 March 1982 [10 days before the invasion], the Ministry of Foreign Affairs expressed concern at news of an insult to the Argentine flag at the LADE (Argentine Air Force airline) office in Port Stanley. The Governor reported that on the night of 20/21 March the LADE office had been entered, apparently by someone using a key. A Union flag had been placed over the Argentine flag there and 'Tit for tat, you buggers' written in toothpaste on a desk. In a later incident, during the night of 22/23 March, 'UK OK' was written on two external windows of the LADE office."

Backdrop
Since 1832, Britain has claimed sovereignty over the Falkland Islands in the South Atlantic. On 2 April 1982 Argentina invaded the Falklands and took possession of Port Stanley.

The Book
How did Britain come to have sovereignty over a small group of islands over 8,000 miles away? What were the events leading up to the Argentine invasion, and why was Britain caught so unprepared? What were the logistical problems involved in mounting a campaign to retake these islands? And how were feelings expressed about this extraordinary event?

These are just some of the issues which are dealt with by the archive material in this uncovered edition. Starting with the official government history of the Falkland Islands (from 1592, when the islands were first sighted), the book then gives the full text of Lord Franks' report, who was appointed in 1982 to investigate the events leading up to the invasion, and to review the way in which the Government discharged its responsibilities. A full description of the operation as submitted to Parliament is included, and also the text of some famous debates in the House of Commons during this turbulent period, featuring interchanges between Margaret Thatcher and the leaders of the other parties.

ISBN 0 11 702458 9   Price £6.99

King Guezo of Dahomey, 1850–52

"Retiring to our seats, the King insisted on our viewing the place of sacrifice. Immediately under the royal canopy were six or eight executioners, armed with large knives, grinning horribly; the mob now armed with clubs and branches, yelled furiously, calling upon the King to 'feed them – they were hungry'. . . When it was all over, at 3 pm, we were permitted to retire. At the foot of the ladder in the boats and baskets lay the bleeding heads. It is my duty to describe; I leave exposition to the reader."

Backdrop
In 1807, the British Parliament outlawed the trade in slaves, followed in 1833 by an Act to abolish the institution of slavery. However, in 1850, the slave trade was alive and well on the west coast of Africa.

The Book
The fact that Africans were still being sold into slavery in the mid-19th century was partly due to the reluctance of both the merchants and the African chiefs to desist. King Guezo was one of these African chiefs who profited by selling captives taken during tribal wars. Although he was very friendly towards the British, counting Queen Victoria as one of his most revered friends, he was reluctant to give up his war-like habits. With 18,000 royal wives, an army composed in part of 3,000 Amazon women, and a warrior-like reputation to maintain, he could see little attraction in farming as an alternative lifestyle. For entertainment, he would regularly indulge in human sacrifice.

Lord Palmerston was the Foreign Secretary who charged the British Consul in west Africa with the unenviable task of persuading the African chiefs to give up their lucrative trade. Just how the British managed to coerce the chiefs into abandoning this practice is revealed in fresh and fascinating detail by these contemporary despatches. They provide an astonishing glimpse of the customs and way of life in Africa some 150 years ago, as told by the people who were there.

ISBN 0 11 702460 0   Price £6.99

War 1939: Dealing with Adolf Hitler

"Herr Hitler asserted that I did not care how many Germans were being slaughtered in Poland. This gratuitous impugnment of the humanity of His Majesty's Government and of myself provoked a heated retort on my part and the remainder of the interview was of a somewhat stormy character."

The Backdrop
As he presided over the rebuilding of a Germany shattered and humiliated after World War I, opinion regarding Hitler and his intentions was divided and the question of whether his ultimate aim was military domination by no means certain.

The Book
Sir Nevile Henderson, the British ambassador in Berlin in 1939, describes here, in his report to Parliament, the failure of his mission and the events leading up to the outbreak of war. He tells of his attempts to deal with both Hitler and von Ribbentrop to maintain peace and gives an account of the changes in German foreign policy regarding Poland. The second part of the book contains documents concerning German-Polish relations up to September 1939.

ISBN 0 11 702411 2   Price £6.99

D Day to VE Day: General Eisenhower's Report, 1944–45

"During the spring of 1945, as the sky grew darker over Germany, the Nazi leaders had struggled desperately, by every means in their power, to whip their people into a last supreme effort to stave off defeat, hoping against hope that it would be possible, if only they could hold out long enough, to save the day by dividing the Allies. Blinded as they were by their own terror and hatred of 'Bolshevism', they were incapable of understanding the strength of the bond of common interest existing between Britain, the United States and the Soviet Union."

Backdrop

In 1944 the Allies were poised to launch an attack against Hitler's German war machine. The planning and timing were crucial. In February, General Eisenhower was appointed Supreme Commander of the Allied Operations in Europe.

The Book

The book is Dwight D. Eisenhower's personal account of the Allied invasion of Europe, from the preparations for the D-Day landings in Normandy, France, to the final assault across Germany. He presents a story of a far more arduous struggle than is commonly portrayed against an enemy whose tenacity he admired and whose skills he feared. It is a tactical account of his understanding of enemy manoeuvres, and his attempts to counter their actions. The formality of the report is coloured by many personal touches, and the reader senses Eisenhower's growing determination to complete the task. Hindsight would have had the general take more notice of Russian activity, but that this was not obvious to him is one of the fascinations of such a contemporary document.

ISBN 0 11 702451 1   Price £6.99

Bloody Sunday, 1972: Lord Widgery's Report

"No order and no training can ensure that a soldier will always act wisely, as well as bravely and with initiative. The individual soldier ought not to have to bear the burden of deciding whether to open fire in confusion such as prevailed on 30 January. In the conditions prevailing in Northern Ireland, however, this is often inescapable."

Backdrop

Northern Ireland forms part of the United Kingdom, and the Protestant majority of its population generally supports political union with Great Britain. However, many of the Roman Catholic minority would prefer union with the Republic of Ireland. This division has sparked much of the conflict between the two communities. In 1969, a British Army peace-keeping force was established in Northern Ireland.

The Book

On Sunday 30 January 1972, a protest march organised by the Northern Ireland Civil Rights Association took place in Londonderry, Northern Ireland, in the area of the Bogside and Creggan Estate. During the afternoon of that march, 13 civilians were killed by British soldiers, and another 13 were injured. As a result, a tribunal was appointed to inquire into the events which led up to this tragic loss of life. Heading the inquiry was Lord Widgery. This uncovered edition is the text of his report.

ISBN 0 11 702405 8   Price £6.99

The Irish Uprising, 1914–21: Papers from the British Parliamentary Archive

"Captain Bowen-Colthurst adopted the extraordinary, and indeed almost meaningless, course of taking Mr Sheehy Skeffington with him as a 'hostage'. He had no right to take Mr Sheehy Skeffington out of the custody of the guard for this or any other purpose, and he asked no one's leave to do so. . . . Before they left the barracks Mr Sheehy Skeffington's hands were tied behind his back and Captain Bowen-Colthurst called upon him to say his prayers. Upon Mr Sheehy Skeffington refusing to do so Captain Bowen-Colthurst ordered the men of his party to take their hats off and himself uttered a prayer, the words of it being: 'O Lord God, if it shall please thee to take away the life of this man, forgive him for Christ's sake.'"

Backdrop

In 1914 it was still the case that the whole of Ireland was part of Great Britain, under the dominion of the King, and Irish constituencies were represented in the British Parliament.

The Book

This book contains five remarkable documents published by the British Government between 1914 and 1921, relating to the events leading up to the partition of Ireland in 1921. In the first, a report is made into the shooting of civilians following a landing of arms at Howth outside Dublin. The second is of the papers discovered relating to the activities of Sinn Fein and particularly of Sir Roger Casement. The third is the government inquiry into the Easter Rising of 1916. The fourth describes the treatment of three journalists by the British Army shortly after the uprising, and the last is an exchange of correspondence between Eamon de Valera and David Lloyd George prior to the Anglo-Irish Treaty of 1921.

ISBN 0 11 702415 5 Price £6.99

British Battles of World War I, 1914–15

*"The effect of these poisonous gases was so virulent as to render the whole
of the line held by the French Division incapable of any action at all. It
was at first impossible for anyone to realise what had actually happened.
The smoke and fumes hid everything from sight, and hundreds of men
were thrown into a comatose or dying condition, and within an hour the
whole position had to be abandoned, together with about 50 guns."*

Backdrop
On 4 August 1914, Britain declared war on Germany. Germany
had already invaded Belgium and France and was progressing
towards Paris.

The Book
These are the despatches from some of the battles of the first two
years of World War I. They include action in northern France,
Germany, Gallipoli, and even as far afield as the Cocos Islands in
the Indian Ocean. They describe the events of battle, the
tremendous courage, the huge losses, and the confusions and difficulties of war. These startling accounts, which were written by
the generals at the front, were first published in the "London
Gazette", the official newspaper of Parliament.

ISBN 0 11 702447 3   Price £6.99

Lord Kitchener and Winston Churchill: The Dardanelles Commission Part I, 1914–15

"The naval attack on the Narrows was never resumed. It is difficult to understand why the War Council did not meet between 19th March and 14th May. The failure of the naval attack showed the necessity of abandoning the plan of forcing the passage of the Dardanelles by purely naval operation. The War Council should then have met and considered the future policy to be pursued."

Backdrop

The Dardanelles formed part of the main southern shipping route to Russia, and was of great military and strategic importance. However, it had long been recognised by the British naval and military authorities that any attack on the Dardanelles would be an operation fraught with great difficulties.

The Book

During the early stages of World War I, Russia made a plea to her allies to make a demonstration against the Turks. So attractive was the prize of the Dardanelles to the British generals, notably Lord Kitchener, that this ill-fated campaign was launched. Just how powerful an influence Kitchener was to exert over the War Council, and just how ill-prepared the Allies were to conduct such an attack, are revealed in dramatic detail in the report of this Commission.

The book covers the first part of the Commission's report. It deals with the origin, inception and conduct of operations in the Dardanelles from the beginning of the war in August 1914 until March 1915, when the idea of a purely naval attack was abandoned.

ISBN 0 11 702423 6   Price £6.99

Defeat at Gallipoli: The Dardanelles Commission Part II, 1915–16

"It has been represented ... that from a military point of view, the Dardanelles Expedition, even if unsuccessful, was justified by the fact that it neutralised or contained a large number of Turkish troops who otherwise would have been free to operate elsewhere. Lord Kitchener estimated this number as being nearly 300,000. But in containing the Turkish force, we employed ... a total of at least 400,000. Our casualties amounted to 31,389 killed, 78,749 wounded and 9,708 missing, making a total of 119,846. The expedition also involved heavy financial expenditure and the employment of a considerable naval force."

Backdrop
The naval attempt by the British to force the Dardanelles was abandoned in March 1915. Rather than losing face, the military commanders decided to send a large army to the area.

The Book
Picking up the story from where the earlier volume, *Lord Kitchener and Winston Churchill*, left off, this second part of the Dardanelles Commission's report deals with the disastrous military campaign to capture the Gallipoli Peninsula using ground forces. As the story unfolds, we learn how the Allies were unable to make any headway against an enemy who was well prepared and well positioned. Within a few months the Allies had suffered a humiliating defeat, and thousands of men had lost their lives. The realisation of the government's incompetence in handling this affair was instrumental in the removal of Herbert Asquith as Prime Minister in December 1916.

ISBN 0 11 702455 4   Price £6.99

Florence Nightingale and the Crimea, 1854–55

"By an oversight, no candles were included among the stores brought to the Crimea. Lamps and wicks were brought but not oil. These omissions were not supplied until after possession had been taken of Balaklava, and the purveyor had an opportunity of purchasing candles and oil from the shipping and the dealers in the town."

Backdrop

The British Army arrived in the Crimea in 1854, ill-equipped to fight a war in the depths of a Russian winter.

The Book

The hospital service for wounded soldiers during the Crimean War was very poor and became the subject of concern, not just in the army, but also in the press. "The Times" was publishing letters from the families of soldiers describing the appalling conditions. This embarrassed the government, but even more it irritated the army, which did not know how to cope with such open scrutiny of its activities.

The book is a collection of extracts from government papers published in 1855 and 1856. Their selection provides a snapshot of events at that time. In particular they focus on the terrible disaster that was the Charge of the Light Brigade, and the inadequate provisions that were made for the care of the sick and wounded. The documents relating to the hospitals at Scutari include evidence from Florence Nightingale herself.

ISBN 0 11 702425 2   Price £6.99

D Day to VE Day: General Eisenhower's Report, 1944–45

"During the spring of 1945, as the sky grew darker over Germany, the Nazi leaders had struggled desperately, by every means in their power, to whip their people into a last supreme effort to stave off defeat, hoping against hope that it would be possible, if only they could hold out long enough, to save the day by dividing the Allies. Blinded as they were by their own terror and hatred of 'Bolshevism', they were incapable of understanding the strength of the bond of common interest existing between Britain, the United States and the Soviet Union."

Backdrop
In 1944 the Allies were poised to launch an attack against Hitler's German war machine. The planning and timing were crucial. In February, General Eisenhower was appointed Supreme Commander of the Allied Operations in Europe.

The Book
The book is Dwight D. Eisenhower's personal account of the Allied invasion of Europe, from the preparations for the D-Day landings in Normandy, France, to the final assault across Germany. He presents a story of a far more arduous struggle than is commonly portrayed against an enemy whose tenacity he admired and whose skills he feared. It is a tactical account of his understanding of enemy manoeuvres, and his attempts to counter their actions. The formality of the report is coloured by many personal touches, and the reader senses Eisenhower's growing determination to complete the task. Hindsight would have had the general take more notice of Russian activity, but that this was not obvious to him is one of the fascinations of such a contemporary document.

ISBN 0 11 702451 1 Price £6.99

The Amritsar Massacre: General Dyer in the Punjab, 1919

"We feel that General Dyer, by adopting an inhuman and un-British method of dealing with subjects of His Majesty the King-Emperor, has done great disservice to the interest of British rule in India. This aspect it was not possible for the people of the mentality of General Dyer to realise."

Backdrop

At the time of the events described, India was under British rule. Indians had fought alongside the British in World War I, and had made tremendous financial contributions to the British war effort. Mahatma Gandhi was the leader of the Indian National Congress party, which was seeking independence from the British Empire.

The Book

This is the story of the action taken by Brigadier-General Dyer at Amritsar in the Punjab in 1919. Faced with insurrection in support of Mahatma Gandhi, the British Army attempted to restore order. General Dyer, on arriving in the troubled city of Amritsar, issued an order banning any assembly of more than four people. Consequently, when he discovered a large crowd gathered together during a cattle fair, he took the astonishing action of shooting more than three hundred unarmed people. Regarding the subsequent native obedience as a satisfactory result, he was surprised to find himself removed from command a year later, and made lengthy representations to Parliament.

ISBN 0 11 702412 0   Price £6.99

The Siege of the Peking Embassy, 1900

"I cannot conclude this despatch without saying a word of praise respect-
ing the ladies of all nationalities who so ably and devotedly assisted the
defence, notwithstanding the terrible shadow which at all times hung over
the legation—a shadow which the never-ceasing rattle of musketry and
crash of round shot and shell and the diminishing number of defenders
rendered ever present. They behaved with infinite patience and cheerful-
ness, helping personally in the hospital or, in making sandbags and
bandages, and in assisting in every possible way the work of defence.
Especially commended are two young ladies—Miss Myers and Miss
Daisy Brazier—who daily filtered the water for the hospital, in tropical
heat, and carried it with bullets whistling and shells bursting in the trees
overhead." Sir Claude MacDonald

Backdrop

The Boxer movement in China was a secret society which
preached hatred of foreigners. By the spring of 1900, this movement was out of control. On 9 June, the Boxers launched their
first attack against foreign property in Peking by burning down
the racecourse. On 19 June, all foreigners were ordered to evacu-
ate Peking within 24 hours. The order was not complied with.

The Book

As events worsened for the diplomats and their families in
Peking, Sir Claude MacDonald, the British ambassador, wired the
Admiralty in Taku to request the immediate despatch of a relief
force. Just how that relief force fared, and how the hundreds of
diplomats and their families who were stranded inside the
Legation buildings coped with the rigours of the siege, are the
subject of the diplomatic papers presented in this book. The central part of the story is the gripping diary of events kept by Sir
Claude MacDonald.

ISBN 0 11 702456 2   Price £6.99

The Russian Revolution, 1917

"It is the general opinion in Ekaterinburg that the Empress, her son, and four daughters were not murdered, but were despatched on the 17th July to the north or the west. The story that they were burnt in a house seems to be an exaggeration of the fact that in a wood outside the town was found a heap of ashes, apparently the result of burning a considerable amount of clothing. At the bottom of the ashes was a diamond, and, as one of the Grand Duchesses is said to have sewn a diamond into the lining of her cloak, it is supposed that the clothes of the Imperial family were burnt there."

Backdrop

By November 1917 Russia had lost more than twenty million people in the war. Lenin's Bolshevik party had overthrown the Tsar and had called for an end to all capitalist governments.

The Book

Government files contain a number of detailed documents describing the nature of the Bolshevik Revolution and the government of Lenin, which was observed to be not only abhorrent but also menacing because of the international implications. The book is compiled from two of these files, one of which describes the events leading up to the revolution and how the Bolsheviks came to power in October 1917. The other contains a series of eye-witness accounts of the frightening days of the Bolshevik regime from the summer of 1918 to April 1919.

ISBN 0 11 702424 4   Price £6.99

The Siege of Kars, 1855

"We had, up to that date, suffered from cold, want of sufficient clothing, and starvation, without a murmur escaping from the troops. They fell dead at their posts, in their tents, and throughout the camp as brave men should who cling to their duty through the slightest glimmering of hope of saving a place entrusted to their custody. From the day of their glorious victory on 29th September, they had not tasted animal food, and their nourishment consisted of two-fifths of a ration of bread and the roots of grass, which they scarcely had the strength to dig for; yet night and day they stood to their arms, their wasted frames showing the fearful effects of starvation, but their sparkling eye telling me what they would do were the enemy to attack them again." W. F. Williams

Backdrop

In 1855, while the British Army was fighting alongside the French and the Turkish armies in the Crimean War, a little-known but serious siege was taking place in the city of Kars in eastern Turkey. Set within mountains and overlooking a gorge, Kars is a natural fortress, but its possession by the Turks was threatened by the Russians.

The Book

During the Crimean War, the British were giving aid to the Turkish army by lending them generals to help organise and strengthen their garrisons. General Williams had arrived in Kars in September 1854, having been appointed British Military Commissioner with the Turkish Army in Asia. He soon began organising the troops there, although his repeated requests for supplies and reinforcements were met with delay and obfuscation. These despatches concerning the siege of Kars date from May 1855. Their unfolding tells a sorry tale of heroism and frustrated hope.

ISBN 0 11 702454 6   Price £6.99